'HOLE NUMBERS'

and other practical investigations

A RESOURCE BOOK FOR MATHEMATICS TEACHERS

Stephen Bell, Peter Brown and Steven Buckley

CAMBRIDGE
UNIVERSITY PRESS

Published by the Press Syndicate of the University of Cambridge
The Pitt Building, Trumpington Street, Cambridge CB2 1RP
40 West 20th Street, New York, NY 10011-4211, USA
10 Stamford Road, Oakleigh, Victoria 3166, Australia

First published 1992

Printed in Great Britain at the University Press, Cambridge

A catalogue record for this book is available from the British Library.

ISBN 0 521 40645 5

CONTENTS

INTRODUCTION

The demands of a modern mathematics scheme coupled with the requirements of the National Curriculum suggest that both investigational and practical work are necessary and desirable additions to any good course. There are books that give suggestions and ideas on how to bring this line of teaching into the classroom but most of them are designed to help pupils to prepare for the GCSE investigational and practical work. This book is to bridge the gap between early primary and late secondary levels and to develop styles of thinking and recording.

Although the National Curriculum sets out what is to be taught and at what stage it is 'appropriate', the teachers still have the flexibility to develop topics in their own way and to suit particular sets of pupils.

For example attainment target 2 (Number) level 3 states that pupils should be able to 'read, write and order numbers to at least 1000; use the knowledge that the position of a digit indicates its value'. Many questions can be set to indicate a particular pupil's level of understanding. The 'traditional' type of question may be: which is bigger, 321 or 576? What is the value of the digit 5 in the number 352? The 'more modern' type of questions may be: choose three different digits. How many numbers can you make using the three digits you have chosen? What is the biggest number you can make? Describe how you make the biggest number from any set of three digits.

Both types of question fit in with the National Curriculum requirements and have their particular value giving the teacher control over the types and style of approach.

Even though pupils may be at different stages in their development, questions may be tackled by a group. The question 'How many ways can you make 16?' covers for example two numbers, three numbers,…, addition, subtraction, multiplication (factors); the pupils' answers will reflect their mathematical experience and abilities.

Teachers can continue to use the investigational and practical work in all areas of mathematics but the National Curriculum has set out one specific attainment target which is concerned directly with practical and investigational work.

AT1 Using and applying mathematics
Pupils should make use of knowledge, skills and understanding outlined in the programmes and study in practical tasks, in real life problems, and to investigate within mathematics itself.

The tasks in this book are intended to cover the work in this attainment target from level 2 to 7 but they will obviously be of value to other attainment targets. The book itself is designed to help teachers of pupils in the age range of 9 to 14 years to offer and develop a course of interest and value within the limits of the National Curriculum. It should give pupils a good working knowledge of the skills and techniques required in preparation for their later GCSE coursework programme.

The main aims of the tasks in the book are to strengthen the pupils' basic organisational skills: planning, systematic searching, the simplification of questions, recording, grouping and tabulating, looking for patterns and relationships, checking, and at a higher level the skills of: generalising, testing, predicting, interpreting and analysing, extending, communication. It is hoped that teachers will find this book a useful addition to their resources and an opportunity to increase the amount of variety in lessons.

USING THE BOOK

This book consists of 28 photocopiable problem sheets for pupils backed up by notes and solutions for the teacher, plus five assessment tasks.

The pupils' problem sheets are written in four sections. The first section, boxed and headed 'Challenge', sets out the situation and the problem to be studied, which takes the form of an open question to be investigated.

The second section, 'Ideas', gives suggestions and explanations which help pupils to answer the open question in the problem. Many important techniques are used and developed, particularly the skills which the pupils need to start to tackle the question – for example, ideas about the use of simple equipment, how a question can be simplified and broken down.

The third section, 'Development', is a series of notes and questions for pupils to answer. These give the problem more structure and help pupils new to this type of question to gain confidence.

The fourth section, 'Extension', takes the form of an open question which allows pupils to apply the techniques they have learned to new and more difficult situations. Some of the questions are particularly difficult and the teacher should fully consider the questions before presenting them to the pupils, some being appropriate for only the very able pupils.

Presentation of work

Teachers must first decide whether to present the tasks to individuals as a supplement to an individual learning scheme or to a group of pupils. It is felt that the group approach is particularly useful as it adds variety to the lessons and the opportunity for increasing pupil/pupil and pupil/teacher communication. When pupils work in small groups they have the opportunity to communicate with each other to test and express their understanding of the problem. This gives pupils a chance to contribute to the final answer for the group, whether it is recorded individually or as a group. The discussion within the group makes communication with the teacher much easier for most children.

Pupils are required by the GCSE boards to learn the technique of answering investigational questions individually. Some teachers may find that some of the tasks in this book can be set to pupils to work through by themselves. There are four ways in which the problems can be presented.

1   A particular problem sheet can be presented as a whole with all four sections. If this is to be done, the layout of the sheet must be made clear to the pupils; that is, the boxed section is the overall aim of the investigation but the second and third sections help them to answer the main question. The whole sheet must be read first!

2   It may be wise to present only the first three sections initially. The extension section may then be given when the main section has been successfully completed. The fact that the extension is not presented with the main problem may give the pupils an opportunity to extend the question in their own way and will result in a greater variety of extension and provide a valuable and interesting experience for the pupils.

3 The challenge and ideas sections could be presented without the development section. This makes the problem more open but gives the pupils some ideas about how to tackle the problem without leading them through the step-by-step approach of the development section.

4 Another method of presentation is to give the boxed section by itself as this allows the pupils to develop their own methods for tackling problems. Pupils must be familiar with problem-solving techniques before this method is used or else they will not have sufficient confidence to make significant progress. If this method is used, the ideas and development sections could then be seen as 'hints' to be used by the teacher during discussion, care being taken not to lead pupils away from other valid approaches. The ideas and development sections could also be used by the teacher as a basis for class discussion at the start of a problem or to pull ideas together at the appropriate moment.

Each of these methods has its own merits and pupils should experience the four approaches.

The teachers' notes

Each task is backed up by a section of teachers' notes which are broken down into:

National Curriculum attainment targets

This section indicates the relevant statements of attainment of the National Curriculum which apply to the task. For example, 'Sloppy Shelves' lists

AT1/4a, b, c, d

AT3/4a, b

AT3/5d

This means that the task encourages the pupils to 'make general statements about patterns' (the first statement at level 4 in attainment target 3). With attainment target 1, although a specific level has been given, the skill a pupil shows may span a range of levels and so the assessment of pupils' work must take this into account.

Preknowledge

This notes what is considered to be *essential* before a task can be adequately tackled.

Skills to be developed

These fall into two categories: the practical/investigational techniques, and the specific mathematical skills such as recognising that squares can be drawn at different angles.

Equipment

This is the equipment which is considered to be essential. Try to ensure that other equipment and materials are freely available for all tasks, so that pupils are not inhibited from developing their own ideas.

Solution

The answers given are really for teachers' use. They are meant to be concise and accurate but will be different from pupils' answers. This difference is important because a pupil may give an answer which is more detailed and includes extra information, and care must be taken not to dismiss an answer because it does not have as high a level of algebra as used in this book. The extension section usually allows pupils who are interested an opportunity to develop the theme in greater depth; some of these questions can only be given an approximate answer whilst others cannot be given a single solution because of the possible variety of approaches.

Discussion points

An important aspect of investigational work that should be emphasised in lessons is the careful organisation of information and the accurate, structured recording of results. The questions in this book are organised in a way which develops these skills. The teacher needs to emphasise and illustrate the processes (organised search, holding variables constant while altering others) in the feedback to the pupils in all the problems. The discussion points listed with solutions are additional to these general points. They are points which are particularly important to the individual problem. Some of these may be brought in as the pupils tackle the problem but they should always be emphasised in the feedback.

Flowchart

The order in which the problems are tackled is extremely important as some of the later problems are dependent upon familiarity with some of the skills learned from earlier questions.

Problems 1 to 4 are at level 3, problems 5 to 15 are at level 4, 16 to 22 are at level 5, 23 to 26 at level 6 and 27 and 28 at level 7.

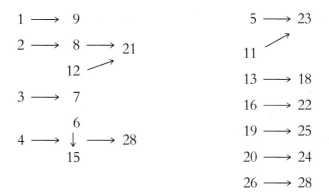

The exact National Curriculum attainment targets covered by each task are summarised in the following reference grid.

National Curriculum reference grid to statements of attainment

NATIONAL CURRICULUM ATTAINMENT TARGETS	1	2	3	4	5
1 Reflection Symmetry	3c			3b	
2 Numbers That Make Numbers	3b 3c	3a 3b 3c 4a			
3 Making Shapes	3a 3b 3c			2a 4a	
4 Annie Ant	3c 4b			5c	
5 Lego Worms	4a 4b 4c 4d	4a 4b 5b			
6 Pentiles	4a 4b			4a	
7 Counted Out	4c 4d	4a 4b	4a 4b 5a		
8 Reflective Flags	4a 4b 4c			3b 4a 5b	
9 A Mass of Test Papers	4a 4b 4c	4a 4b 4c 4e 5d			
10 Pop-up Card	4a			4a 5a	
11 Sloppy Shelves	4a 4b 4c 4d		4a 4b 5b		
12 Building Blocks	4a 4b 4c 4d	4a	4a	4a	
13 Finding Squares	5a 5b 5c		4a	4a 5b	
14 Mind Reading	4b 4c		4a 4b		

The tasks in this book cover all the attainment targets of the National Curriculum at most of the levels from 3 to 8. They are not, however, specifically written for attainment targets 2 to 5 and in general they cannot be used directly for assessing them, although a pupil's solution to a task may give supporting evidence that one of these attainment targets at a given level is fully understood. It must be emphasised that the level of work covered by a particular task in terms of attainment targets 2 to 5 is very important when assessing attainment target 1.

Assessing attainment target 1

Assessing a pupil's abilities in this attainment target is particularly difficult. To do it effectively it is necessary to break down the National Curriculum statements into two further categories – general statements and specific statements.

The *general statements* are those which are found across several levels of the programmes of study and are not clearly defined: for example, 'selecting the materials and mathematics to use for a task' appears, though worded slightly differently, at levels 2 to 7.

The *specific statements* cover the different investigational and practical skills which should be used at a given level, ranging from AT1 level 3d ('checking results and considering whether they are sensible') to AT1 level 7 ('following a chain of mathematical reasoning; spotting inconsistencies').

Here is the breakdown of the levels of AT 1 into general skills and specific skills:

LEVEL	PROGRAMME OF STUDY	GENERAL	SPECIFIC
3	• selecting the materials and the mathematics to use for a task using alternative approaches to overcome difficulties	selecting the materials and the mathematics to use for a task using alternative approaches to overcome difficulties	
	• explaining work and recording findings systematically	explaining work and recording findings systematically	
	• investigating and testing predictions and general statements		investigating and testing predictions and general statements
	• checking results, considering whether they are sensible		checking results, considering whether they are sensible
4	• selecting the materials and the mathematics to use for a task when the information leaves opportunities for choice; planning work methodically	selecting the materials and the mathematics to use for a task when the information leaves opportunities for choice	planning work methodically

LEVEL	PROGRAMME OF STUDY	GENERAL	SPECIFIC
	• recording findings and presenting them in oral, written or visual form	recording findings and presenting them in oral, written or visual form	
	• using examples to test statements or definitions		using examples to test statements or definitions
	• making generalisations or simple hypotheses		making generalisations or simple hypotheses
5	• selecting the materials and the mathematics to use for a task; checking there is sufficient information; working methodically and reviewing progress	selecting the materials and the mathematics to use for a task	checking there is sufficient information; working methodically and reviewing progress
	• breaking tasks into smaller more manageable tasks		breaking tasks into smaller more manageable tasks
	• interpreting mathematical information presented in oral, written or visual form	interpreting mathematical information presented in oral, written or visual form	
	• generalising from a number of particular examples and carrying out simple tests		generalising from a number of particular examples and carrying out simple tests
6	• designing a task and selecting the mathematics and resources; checking information and obtaining any that is missing; using 'trial and improvement' methods	designing a task and selecting the mathematics and resources; checking information and obtaining any that is missing	using 'trial and improvement' methods
	• examining and presenting findings using oral, written or visual forms	examining and presenting findings using oral, written or visual forms	
	• making and testing generalisations and simple hypotheses; defining and reasoning in simple contexts with some precision		making and testing generalisations and simple hypotheses; defining and reasoning in simple contexts with some precision
7	• following new lines of investigation using alternative methods to overcome difficulties;	devising a mathematical task; working methodically within an agreed structure; using	following new lines of investigation using alternative methods to overcome difficulties;

| | devising a mathematical task; working methodically within an agreed structure; using judgement in the use of given information, using 'trial and improvement' methods and reviewing progress | 'trial and improvement' methods and reviewing progress | using judgement in the use of given information |
| | • following a chain of mathematical reasoning; spotting inconsistencies | | following a chain of mathematical reasoning; spotting inconsistencies |

To assess the general skills the question which must be posed is 'What level of mathematics is the pupil applying?' and this will come from the skills drawn from ATs 2 to 5. In order to do this, any question must be looked at in terms of the skills required to complete the task and the National Curriculum levels linked to the skills. Most of the specific skills are more easily identifiable in a pupil's work, but some may only become apparent from discussions with pupils. It is therefore essential that teachers record the important elements of these discussions.

Here is an example of an assessment task, 'Squares', together with a breakdown of the necessary skills linked to the attainment targets.

This 1 by 1 black square is surrounded by 8 other white squares.

1 How many white squares would be needed to surround this 2 by 2 black square?

2 How many white squares would be needed to surround different sized black squares?

3 Work out how many white squares are needed to surround a 78 by 78 square of black tiles. Explain your answer.

Squares

	Indicators of general skills		Specific skills (AT1)
AT3/3b	Recognising how the pattern continues. The pupil is able to continue the pattern 8, 12, 16, ...	AT1/3a	Drawing further diagrams, correctly counting white squares.
		AT1/3d	Checking the results.
		AT1/3c	Predicting the next number of white tiles and checking by use of a diagram.
AT3/4a	Describe how the pattern is developing: 'As the size of the black square is increased by 1 the number of white tiles increases by 4 because ...'	AT1/4a	Evidence of recording and tabulating results in an orderly manner from diagrams indicates a good level of planning.
AT3/4d	Recognise links between the size of the black square and the number of white tiles by example or machine chain $b \rightarrow \boxed{\times 4} \rightarrow \boxed{+ 4} \rightarrow w$	AT1/4c*	This will come from teacher-presented questions, e.g. 'How many white tiles would be needed to surround a 10 by 10 arrangement?' and a pupil check by drawing.
AT3/5b	To work out the number of white tiles you multiply by 4 for the four sides and add 4 for the corners.	AT1/5a	There is probably insufficient in the question to confirm a pupil's ability at this level.
AT3/5d	Using specific algebraic techniques $b \times 4 + 4 = w$ where $b = ...$ and $w = ...$	AT1/5d	Pupil makes own predictions and checks by drawing.

The task is appropriate to set for pupils working at level 4. It has the flexibility to give indicators of a pupil's ability at level 3 and level 5 but further evidence would probably be required. Clearly a single task would be insufficient to make firm statements about an individual's ability but evidence can be collected from all the other tasks which pupils tackle in less formal situations.

The oral communication between teachers and pupils is very important when assessing the task, especially to ensure that a pupil is predicting and checking results; a process that is very often done 'informally' by pupils. AT1/4c is starred. This indicates that for most pupils evidence of their ability at this specific skill will come only from discussion with the teacher.

The assessment guides indicate what pupils are likely to produce but are not exhaustive. Some pupils may produce relevant solutions which include work not covered in the guide. It will be necessary to match this work to the appropriate attainment targets.

Here are five examples of pupils' solutions to the 'Squares' task annotated with attainment target indicators.

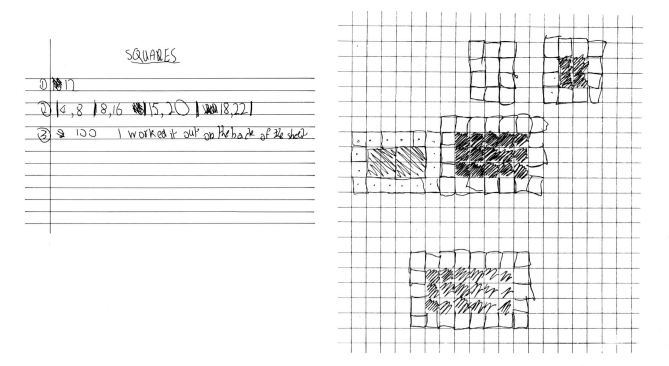

This pupil has misunderstood the question and drawn rectangular arrangements. He has failed to reach level 3. It appears that he requires additional help with AT 3 before progress can be made and specifically with the growth of patterns.

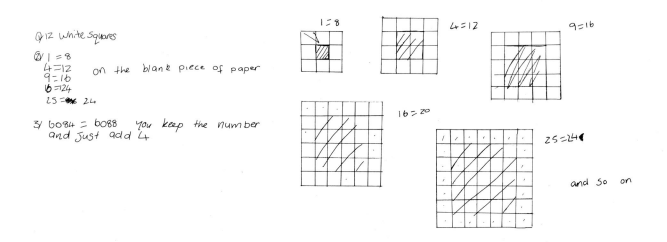

This pupil has tried to link the number of black squares with the number of white squares.

During discussions with the pupil it became clear that she could explain more fully that the number of white squares increased by 4 each time and why it did so. She had therefore successfully completed AT3 4a and 4b and AT1 4a and 4c. This is a level 4 piece of work.

SQUARES

1. You would need 12 white squares to surround the 2 by 2 squares.

2. 12 white tiles would be need to surround different sized black squares.

3. 316 are needed to surround a 78 by 78 square of black tiles. ~~BECAUSE~~ I worked out the answer by drawing little diagrams on squared paper.

3 by 3 = 16
4 by 4 = 80
5 by 5 = 25
6 by 6 = 28
7 by 7 = 32
8 by 8 = 36
9 by 9 = 40
10 by 10 = 44

Every time you get answers like these there's always a 4 in between

```
  78
× 34
 312
+  4
 316
```

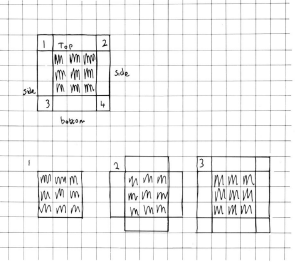

This is a sound piece of work at level 4.

Squares

1. 12

2. To surround different sized black squares, for example say if x means top bottom and sides you need four times x plus four.
The example on the squared paper is a 3 by 3 square surrounded by white squares there is four long strips round it with 3 squares in them and one seperate square at each of the corners. The rule is 4 times x plus four. Underneath the example I have, I have done the example is done in steps

3. 78
778
156 + 4 = 160 + 156 = 316
To surround a 78 by 78 black squares you need 316 white squares because you times 78 by four and then add four.

The relationship has been recognised early and the pupil has not found it necessary to draw diagrams in sequence. This pupil is working at level 5 although a more difficult problem must be set to confirm this.

---

1. 12 Squares

2. Count the number of black squares down one side, multiply your answer by 4 then plus 4 and you have the no of white squares you need to surround it.

3. 316 I got my answer by × by 4 then add 4
(b × 4) + 4 = W

```
  78          312
×  4        +   4
 312          316
  3
```

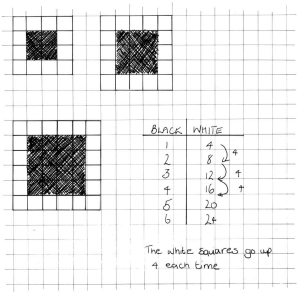

BLACK	WHITE
1	4
2	8
3	12
4	16
5	20
6	24

The white squares go up 4 each time

This pupil has worked through the question in an organised way and is producing work at level 5 standard.

CHALLENGE

Trace these shapes onto card and cut them out.

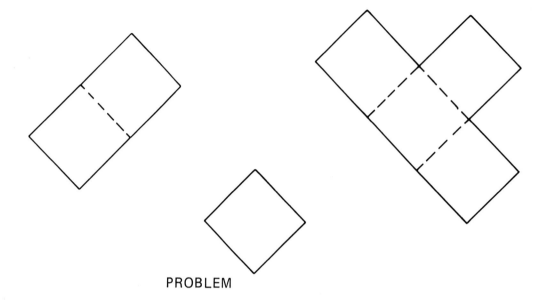

PROBLEM

Use the pieces to make as many shapes as possible which have at least one line of reflection symmetry.

Draw your shapes that have a line of reflection symmetry on squared paper. Make sure that they are different.

Ideas

It is easier to find the most symmetrical designs if you work in an organised manner. You can do this by looking at the symmetry of each shape first, then looking at designs made with pairs of shapes and finally designs made with all three shapes.

Development

1 Start by looking at the individual shapes. Do they have lines of reflection symmetry? If so, copy them onto squared paper and draw in the lines of reflection symmetry.

1

From *'Hole numbers' and other practical investigations* © Cambridge University Press 1992

2 Now look at shapes that can be made with just two pieces. There are different pairs that can be picked. This is one pair.

What shapes with lines of reflection symmetry can be made with these two pieces? Record your shapes on squared paper. Make sure all your shapes are different.

3 Look at the other possible pairs. Make shapes which have reflection symmetry with these pairs.

4 Now look for shapes that can be made with all three pieces.

Extension

Trace these three shapes onto card and cut them out.

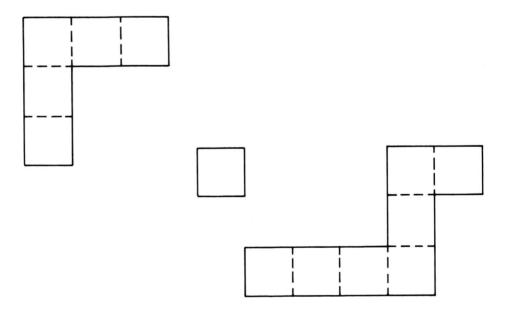

Try to make as many shapes as possible which have at least one line of reflection symmetry. Copy any symmetrical shapes you find onto squared paper. You may turn the shapes over and you must use all three shapes together.

From *'Hole numbers' and other practical investigations* © Cambridge University Press 1992

REFLECTION SYMMETRY – *NOTES*

National Curriculum attainment targets

AT1/3c   AT4/3b

Preknowledge

An understanding of what is meant by the term reflection symmetry
Simple understanding of congruence

Skills to be developed

Making shapes with reflection symmetry
Working in an organised way to find all possibilities

Equipment

Tracing paper   Card   Scissors   Squared paper   Mirrors

Solution

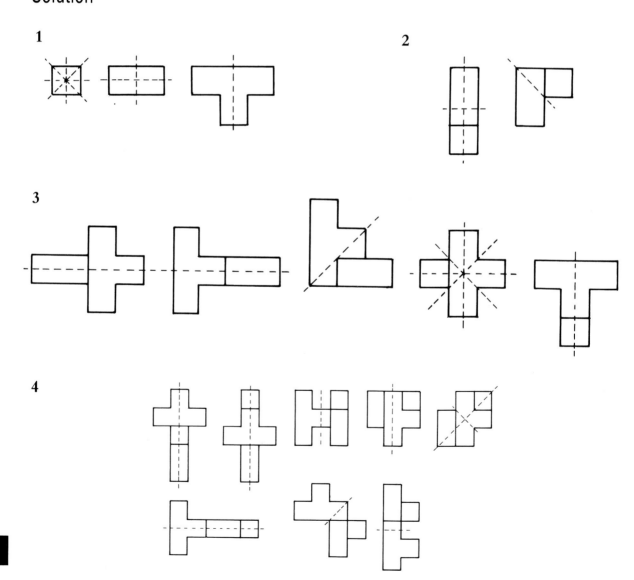

Extension

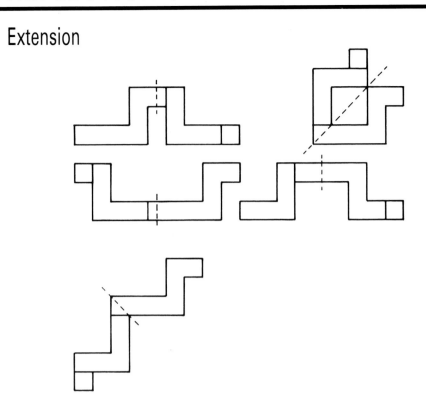

Discussion points

Shapes may have more than one line of symmetry.

Lines of symmetry may not be horizontal and vertical.

Emphasise how to work in an organised manner.

When using all three pieces it is better to place the larger pieces together and then add the third to make a shape with reflection symmetry.

Some designs can be made up from different arrangements of the three pieces.

No restrictions have been placed on the construction of symmetrical designs but the solution only covers shapes which are constructed 'square to square'.

Pupils should be encouraged to identify their own rules of construction.

4

NUMBERS THAT MAKE NUMBERS

CHALLENGE

Which whole numbers can be made from the numbers 1, 2, 3 and 4?

The numbers 1, 2, 3, 4 must be used once and only once each time but the operations (+, −, ×, ÷) and brackets can be used as many times as you like.

TARGETS
15 different numbers   Good!
20 different numbers   Very good!
25 different numbers   Excellent!

Ideas

Here are some examples.

It may be helpful to list 1 to 30 down the left-hand side of your page. Use the right-hand side of the page for working out.

Development

On the right-hand side of the page, play about with the numbers and see what answers you get. Write your solutions next to the appropriate numbers on the left-hand side.

See if you can make other solutions by slightly adjusting the solutions you have already found, for example by changing an 'add 1' to a 'subtract 1'.

Extension

5

Use the numbers 1, 2, 3, 4 to make fractions which are between 0 and 1.

From 'Hole numbers' and other practical investigations © Cambridge University Press 1992

National Curriculum attainment targets

AT1/3b, c   AT2/3a, b, c, 4a

Preknowledge

Ability to add, subtract, multiply and divide numbers

Skills to be developed

The order of operations can be developed with more able pupils; some children will use number chains
Effect of multiplying by 1, etc.
Using knowledge of factors

Equipment

Usual classroom equipment

Solution

Pupils may have other equally valid solutions. Higher numbers can be made.

$1 = 1 \times 2 + 3 - 4$	$11 = 3 \times 2 + 4 + 1$	$21 = (3 + 2) \times 4 + 1$
$2 = 1 + 2 + 3 - 4$	$12 = 4 \times 3 \times (2 - 1)$	$22 = (4 \times 3 - 1) \times 2$
$3 = 1 \times 2 + 4 - 3$	$13 = 3 \times 4 + 2 - 1$	$23 = 4 \times 3 \times 2 - 1$
$4 = 1 + 2 + 4 - 3$	$14 = 3 \times 4 \times 1 + 2$	$24 = 4 \times 3 \times 2 \times 1$
$5 = 1 \times 3 + 4 - 2$	$15 = 3 \times 4 + 2 + 1$	$25 = 4 \times 3 \times 2 + 1$
$6 = 1 + 3 + 4 - 2$	$16 = (4 + 3 + 1) \times 2$	$26 = (4 \times 3 + 1) \times 2$
$7 = (4 - 2) \times 3 + 1$	$17 = (4 + 1) \times 3 + 2$	$27 = (4 \times 2 + 1) \times 3$
$8 = 4 + 3 + 2 - 1$	$18 = (4 + 2) \times 3 \times 1$	$28 = (3 \times 2 + 1) \times 4$
$9 = 3 \times 2 + 4 - 1$	$19 = (3 + 2) \times 4 - 1$	29
$10 = 4 + 3 + 2 + 1$	$20 = (3 + 2) \times 4 \times 1$	$30 = (4 + 1) \times 3 \times 2$

29 cannot be made without using powers or factorials.

Extension

Pupils may try to find: (a) the largest and smallest fractions; (b) fractions equivalent to $\frac{1}{2}$, $\frac{1}{3}$, $\frac{1}{4}$, $\frac{1}{5}$, ...

Discussion points

Make sure pupils notice the effect of multiplying and dividing by 1.
A set of numbers can be generated by subtracting, multiplying by, or adding 1.

Factors can be used to find numbers; for example,
$$18 = 6 \times 3 = (2 + 4) \times 3 \times 1$$
The order of operations is important: $3 + 2 \times 4 + 1 = 12$
is mathematically correct according to the usual convention of 'BODMAS', but pupils may give an answer of 21 if they treat it as a number chain going from left to right, i.e. $(3 + 2) \times 4 + 1 = 21$

CHALLENGE

On the worksheet 'Making Shapes' there are four triangles, A, B, C and D.

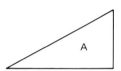 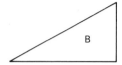 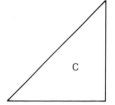 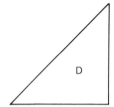

What familiar mathematical shapes can you make from these four triangles? You don't have to use all four triangles at once. Draw and label the shapes you make.

Ideas

If you start by trying to find the shapes with all four triangles it would be difficult. Start by making shapes with just two triangles A and B and then look at other possible groups of triangles; C with D, A with C, and larger groupings.

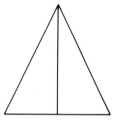

Development

1 Cut out triangles A and B from the worksheet. These two triangles are congruent. Put the two triangles together to make different shapes. Copy the shapes you make onto paper. If you make a special mathematical shape, write down its name. For example, this is an isosceles triangle.

2 Cut out triangles C and D from the worksheet. See what shapes you can make by putting these two triangles together. Don't forget to draw your shapes on paper and write down their names.

3 Try putting shapes A and C together. What shapes can you make?

4 Try making shapes from sets of three – triangles A, B and D or triangles A, C and D.

5 See what shapes you can make by putting all four triangles together.

Extension

Cut out the five pieces making up shape E on the worksheet. See what other shapes you can make from these five pieces.

7

From 'Hole numbers' and other practical investigations © Cambridge University Press 1992

MAKING SHAPES – *NOTES*

National Curriculum attainment targets

AT1/3a, b, c   AT4/2a, 4a

Preknowledge

A basic understanding of shapes and a use of the associated terms

Skills to be developed

Organised searching
Consolidated knowledge of two-dimensional shapes and their classifications
Improvement of spatial awareness

Equipment

Worksheet   Scissors

Solution

1

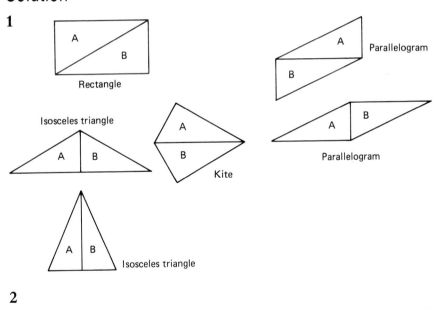

2

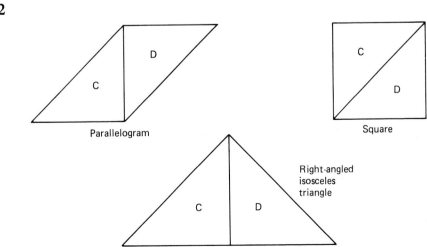

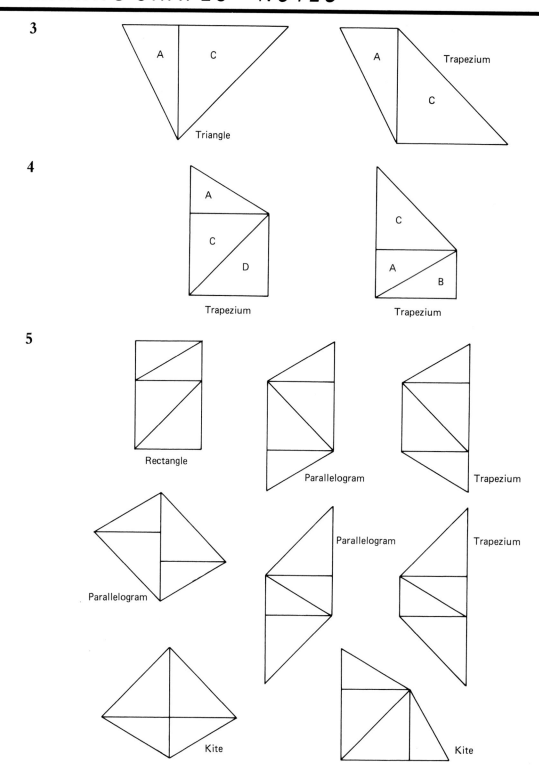

Discussion points

It is important to discuss fully the properties of, and the differences between, the shapes found in order to classify them.

Discuss the rules for forming the shapes; without any restrictions an infinite number of shapes could be made. The most suitable rule is: 'edges must be fully matched to other edges'.

CHALLENGE

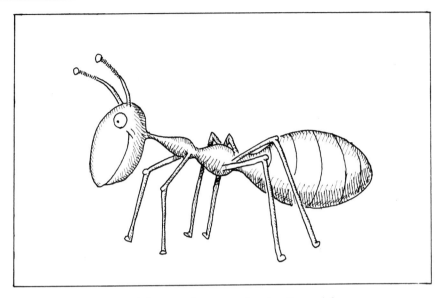

Annie Ant has found an old aquarium at the bottom of someone's garden. The glass is missing so only the metal frame remains.

Annie climbs onto the cuboid frame at corner A as shown on the diagram. She looks around and sees some horseradish at H; a tasty snack.

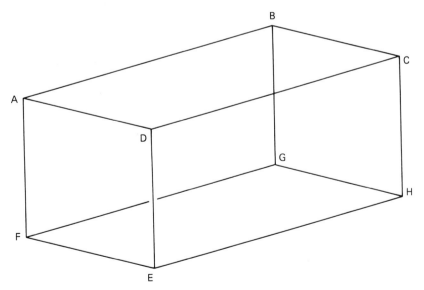

Annie decides to walk to H along the framework. Being a clever ant, she never visits the same corner twice and doesn't climb upwards.

List all the different ways that Annie can get from A to H.

Ideas

Annie starts at A so she could first walk to vertices B, D or F.
Instead of trying to follow the journeys on the cuboid, you could
show them like this:

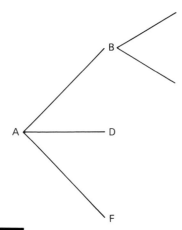

Development

1 Copy this diagram halfway down a piece of paper, starting on
the left-hand side. You are going to need a lot of room to add
further journeys.

2 Suppose Annie went to B; from here she could walk to two
vertices. One of these is C; which is the other? Add these to your
diagram.

3 From C she could travel to H (the end of her journey) or to one
other vertex. Add these to your diagram.

You should now have one complete journey: A, B, C, H. Put a
tick at the end of the line.

4 There are several incomplete journeys. Work through in a similar
way to complete all the different journeys. If you find your
diagram is becoming too cramped, start again but give yourself
more room. It is better to start again and work from a clear
diagram than to work through a muddle and make mistakes!

5 Make a list of all the journeys.

Extension

1 On another trip out, Annie comes across a place where some
people have had a picnic. They were messy eaters and Annie
finds some scraps of food: a piece of apple, a piece of banana, a
piece of cucumber and a piece of date.
List the different orders in which Annie could eat these.

2 Investigate the number of different orders in which Annie can
eat different numbers of pieces of food.

11

From 'Hole numbers' and other practical investigations © Cambridge University Press 1992

National Curriculum attainment targets

AT1/3c, 4b   AT4/5c

Preknowledge

Pupils should be familiar with three-dimensional objects, particularly cuboids, and the associated terms such as vertex, vertices and edges.

Skills to be developed

Development of understanding of movement in three dimensions
Spatial skills – transformation of a three-dimensional figure into a two-dimensional drawing
Introducing the use of a diagram to help list systematically

Equipment

Cuboids can be constructed from pipe-cleaners and straws.

Solution

ABCH	ADEFGH
ABCDEH	ADCH
ABCDEFGH	ADCBGH
ABGH	ADCBGFEH
ABGFEH	AFEH
ADEH	AFGH

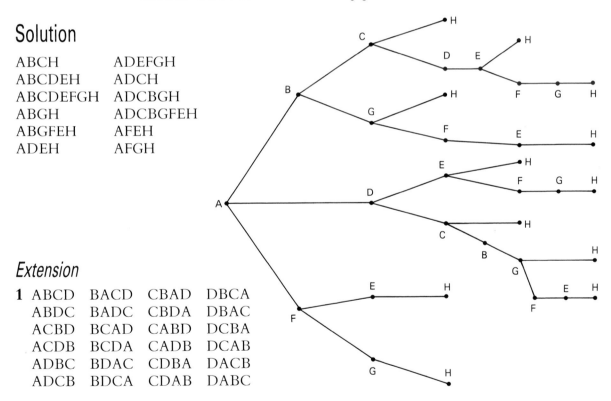

Extension

1

ABCD	BACD	CBAD	DBCA
ABDC	BADC	CBDA	DBAC
ACBD	BCAD	CABD	DCBA
ACDB	BCDA	CADB	DCAB
ADBC	BDAC	CDBA	DACB
ADCB	BDCA	CDAB	DABC

2 If there are *n* different pieces of food, then there are *n*! different orders in which they can be eaten.

Discussion points

The problem shows how a tree diagram assists in listing.

Point out how a three-dimensional object can be represented in two dimensions to simplify a problem.

12

CHALLENGE

Su Ying is playing with her Lego. She has a number of pieces with 6 pins on the top like this.

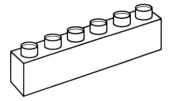

She joins them together to make long worms by connecting the end pin on the top of one piece to the end hole on the bottom of the next piece.

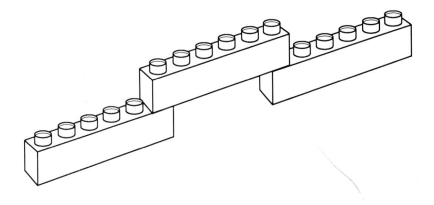

This worm is 3 pieces long and has 16 pins showing.

How many pins will be showing if she makes a worm from 100 pieces?

Ideas

Even if you had 100 6-pin pieces of Lego like Su Ying it would take a long time to make the worm and to count the pins. It is easier to make a short worm and add a piece at a time to make longer worms. Then look for a pattern to help you complete the challenge without making a 100 piece worm.

From 'Hole numbers' and other practical investigations © Cambridge University Press 1992

LEGO WORMS

Development

1 Start with a worm made from one 6-pin piece. How many pins are showing?

2 Now make longer worms by adding one piece at a time. Make at least six different worms to ensure that you have enough information. Keep a record of your results in a table like this.

Pieces used	Pins showing

By doing it in an ordered way, starting with small worms, you should be able to find a pattern.

3 What is the pattern in the 'Pins showing' column of your table?

4 Use this pattern to predict the number of pins showing on a 100 6-pin worm.

5 Find a link between the 'Pieces used' column and the 'Pins showing' column.

6 Use this link to predict the number of pins showing on a 100 piece worm.

Check that your answers to questions 4 and 6 are the same. If they are not, ask your teacher for help.

Extension

1 Using the same 6-pin pieces but overlapping by two pins, try to predict the number of pins showing in a worm 100 pieces long.

2 Investigate worms made from different Lego pieces. Record your results and write down any patterns you notice.

From *'Hole numbers' and other practical investigations* © Cambridge University Press 1992

LEGO WORMS – *NOTES*

National Curriculum attainment targets

AT1/4a, b, c, d   AT3/4a, b, 5b

Preknowledge

Basic number skills

Skills to be developed

Working systematically
Tabulating results in an organised way
Extending sequences to predict further examples
Simple generalisation and use of formula in a written form

Equipment

Lego bricks (6 by 1 pin bricks are a necessity)

Solution

1 Six pins are showing.

2

Pieces used	Pins showing
1	6
2	11
3	16
4	21
5	26
6	31
7	36
8	41

3 As the number of pieces of Lego used increases by 1, the number of pins showing increases by 5.

4 By repeatedly adding 5 to the 'Pins showing' column you eventually get: 'Pieces used' 100, 'Pins showing' 501.

5 The number of pins showing (p) is one more than five times the number of Lego pieces making the worm (w).
$$p = 5w + 1$$

6 Pins showing = $5 \times 100 + 1 = 501$

Extension

1 Using a two-pin overlap,
$$p = 4 \times w + 2$$
so in a 100 piece worm there are 402 pins showing.

2 If the number of pins showing $= p$, the number of pieces used $= w$, the number of pins overlapped $= q$, and the number of pins on one piece $= m$, then
$$p = (m - q)w + q$$

Discussion points

This problem illustrates:
- the importance of simplifying a difficult problem to make it more manageable;
- working in an organised and systematic way;
- the importance of an ordered table to help predict results;
- a generalisation is a better way of predicting an answer than extending a table endlessly.

CHALLENGE

A 'pentile' is a shape made by putting five squares of the same size together edge to edge. ('Pent' means 'five'.)

These arrangements give the **same** pentile.

These are **not** pentiles.

The edges must not overlap.

The squares must fit together edge to edge not corner to corner.

Make as many different shaped pentiles as you can. Draw your pentiles on squared paper. (Check that they are all different.)

Ideas

It helps you to find all the pentiles if you work in an organised way. You can do this by first finding all pentiles with five squares in a row (very easy), then those with four squares in a row (fairly easy), and so on.

It is easier if you cut five squares from squared paper and move these around to find different shapes.

From 'Hole numbers' and other practical investigations © Cambridge University Press 1992

PENTILES

Development

1 How many different shapes can be made by putting five squares in a row?

2 Now put four squares in a row. Think where the fifth square can go. Draw your different shapes on squared paper. Be careful: shapes may look different but might just be reflections or rotations of others.

3 Put three squares in a row and find where the other two squares can go. Don't forget that you already have the shapes with four squares in a row.

4 Now find the shapes with two squares in a row. Make sure that none have more than two squares in any row.

5 Why is it silly to look for shapes with one square in a row?

6 How many different pentiles have you made?

Extension

1 Cut out all your pentiles. On squared paper draw a 20 by 3 rectangle. Try to fit all your pentiles into the rectangle. If you can do it, draw where they go.

2 Try to fit your pentiles into other rectangles which are made up from 60 squares, for example a 12 by 5 rectangle.

From *'Hole numbers' and other practical investigations* © Cambridge University Press 1992

PENTILES – *NOTES*

National Curriculum attainment targets

AT1/4a, b   AT4/4a

Preknowledge

Idea of simple reflections and rotations

Skills to be developed

Strengthening the concept of congruence
Developing a systematic approach to the making of shapes
Strengthening the idea of how shapes fit together

Equipment

Scissors   Squared paper

Solution

1 One way

2

3

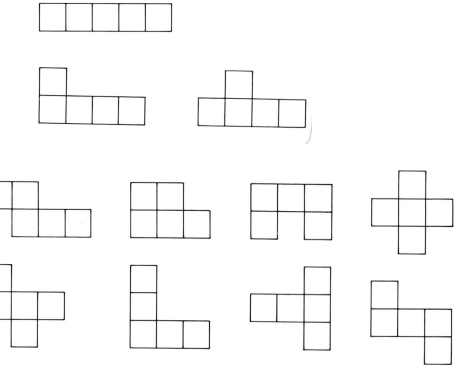

4

PENTILES – *NOTES*

5 Two squares cannot be put together edge to edge in a one-in-a-row arrangement.

6 12

Extension

Pupils may have different arrangements.

1

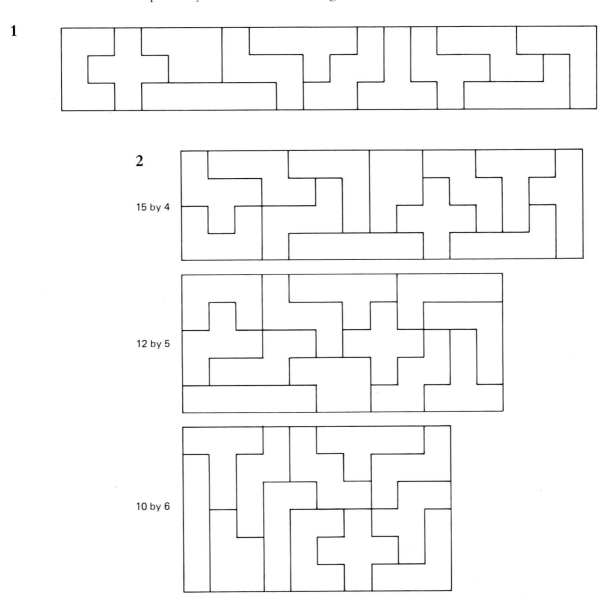

2

15 by 4

12 by 5

10 by 6

Discussion points

Check that the shapes are not reflections or rotations of others already found.

The concept of congruence can be introduced.

Shapes can be turned over in the extension.

It may be interesting to consider how pentiles can be built up from arrangements of 1 square, 2 squares, 3 squares and 4 squares.

COUNTED OUT

CHALLENGE

Can you work out the sum of the first 100 counting numbers
   1 + 2 + 3 + 4 + 5 + ... + 99 + 100 = ?
in less than a minute?

Ideas

Here is a clever way to find the sum of the first six counting
numbers   1 + 2 + 3 + 4 + 5 + 6 = ?

First write down the counting numbers in order of size: 1 + 2 + 3 + 4 + 5 + 6
Then write them down in reverse order: 6 + 5 + 4 + 3 + 2 + 1

The sum is the same for each column: 7 + 7 + 7 + 7 + 7 + 7

You get 6 lots of 7, that is 42.

This is twice the size of the six numbers you started with because it
has been added onto itself. So the sum of the first six counting
numbers is 42 ÷ 2 = 21.
Study the number patterns and use the method to answer the challenge.

Development

1 Use the method to find the sum of the first (a) 8 counting
numbers, (b) 12 counting numbers, (c) 15 counting numbers.
Check your answers by adding each string of numbers.

2 If you were to use this method and write out all the numbers it
would take a long time. However, you don't need to write down
all the numbers in this way. Work out the sum of the first 50
counting numbers without listing all the numbers. Explain your
method fully.

3 What is the sum of the first 75 counting numbers?

4 Write down the rule which helps you to find the sum of any set
of counting numbers starting from 1.

5 Now try the challenge. Don't forget to time yourself.

Extension

1 Try to find the sum of the first 100 numbers in this sequence:
2, 4, 6, 8, ...

2 Try to find the sum of the first 100 numbers in these sequences.
(a) 1, 3, 5, 7, ...   (b) 1, 5, 9, 13, ...   (c) 16, 18, 20, 22,...

3 Can you use this method to work out the sum of the first 100
numbers in all sequences? Make up some sequences of your
own and see if you can.

21

COUNTED OUT – *NOTES*

National Curriculum attainment targets

AT1/4c, d   AT2/4a, b   AT3/4a, b, 5a

Preknowledge

Basic arithmetic
Multiplication as repeated addition
Use of the word 'sum' of numbers
Understanding of arithmetic sequences

Skills to be developed

Ability to find the first ten terms of an arithmetic sequence
Ability to use simple formulas expressed in words

Equipment

Calculator

Solution

Challenge answer: 5050

1 (a) 36 (b) 78 (c) 120

2 The sum of the first 50 counting numbers is 1275. Check the pupils' explanation of the method they used.

3 $\frac{1}{2} \times 75 \times 76 = 2850$

4 The sum of the first n counting numbers is $\frac{1}{2}n(n + 1)$.

5 The answer to the challenge is 5050.

Extension

1 10 100

2 (a) 10 000 (b) 19 900 (c) 11 500

3 The pupil's own-sequence. Only arithmetic progressions can be summed using this method.

Discussion points

The system only works with arithmetic sequences.

Karl Gauss (1777–1855) worked out the answer to the sum of the first 1000 counting numbers when he was nine years old.

There is a link with triangle numbers since the sum of the first six counting numbers is the sixth triangle number.

Sandy Castle found the sales of his flags falling off. They were flagging so badly he decided to bring in a consultant to ask advice on how to raise the standard. After reflecting on the situation for some time, Myra Image came up with the idea of symmetrical black and white square flags.

Sandy's flags were to be made up of 9 small squares like this.

By shading some of the squares he could make flags that were symmetrical, for example:

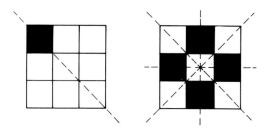

Sandy had to be careful because although some flags looked different at first, they were like some he had already made; they had simply been turned around or over. So

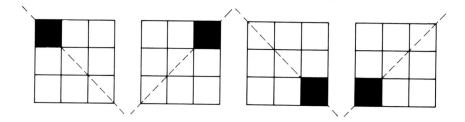

were really all the same.

Find all the different flags Sandy could make by shading in different numbers of small squares in the 3 by 3 square flag. Draw in the lines of reflection symmetry on your arrangements.

There is a worksheet of blank flags which will help you.

From *'Hole numbers' and other practical investigations* © Cambridge University Press 1992

Ideas

There will be many different ways to design Sandy's flags so it is important to work in an organised way. Start by finding the flags which have only one square shaded. It may help if you cut out a shaded square from the bottom of the worksheet; this can be moved around and will avoid drawing unnecessary flags.

Development

1 Find all the different flags that can be made by shading one square. Draw the flags on your worksheet and don't forget to draw in the lines of symmetry.

2 Now look for the symmetrical flags that can be made by shading two squares.

(a) On your worksheet draw a flag like this.

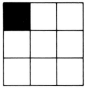

The cut-out shaded square can be moved to different positions in this diagram to help you find some of the flags which have two squares shaded.

This is one position, but it is not a reflective flag!

Record your reflective flags on the worksheet.

(b) Now move the position of your first shaded square.

Find other reflective flags which have two squares shaded by moving your cut-out

(c) Continuing to work in this organised way, find all other two-square reflective flags.

3 Now try to find all the three-square and four-square reflective flags.

4 Predict how many eight-square reflective flags there will be. Check by drawing all the different arrangements.

5 Was your prediction correct? What do you notice about the number of eight-square reflective flags and the number of one-square reflective flags? Can you explain this?

6 How many five-square reflective flags will there be?

7 What is the total number of different reflective flags that can be made?

24

From *'Hole numbers' and other practical investigations* © Cambridge University Press 1992

REFLECTIVE FLAGS – *NOTES*

National Curriculum attainment targets

AT1/4a, b, c   AT4/3b, 4a, 5b

Preknowledge

Understanding of reflective symmetry and some understanding of transformations

Skills to be developed

Strengthening of the concept of reflection symmetry
Organised search to try to ensure that all combinations are considered
Recognising that some results can be found by inference – the idea of a 'negative image'
Organised recording of information

Equipment

Mirrors   Scissors   Worksheet

Solution

1

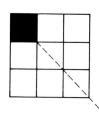 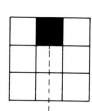 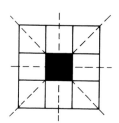

These arrangements do not include rotations of the same design.

2 (a)

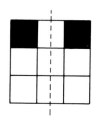 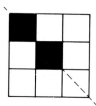 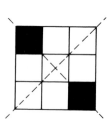

(b)

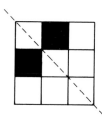 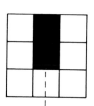 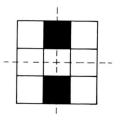

(c) There are no other reflective flags with two squares shaded.

3

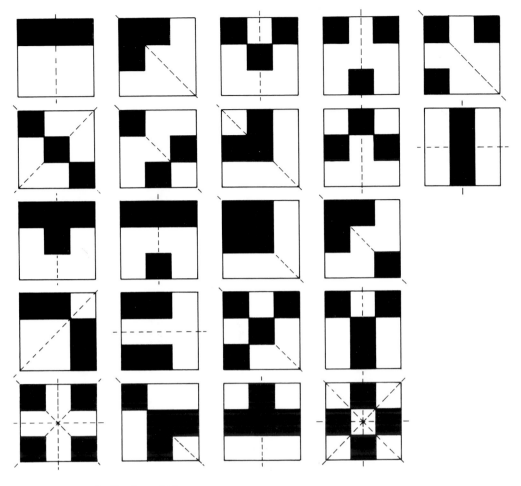

4, 5, 6 and **7**

1 and 8, 2 and 7, 3 and 6, 4 and 5 squares shaded produce the same number of flags because each one of the pairs is a 'negative image' of the other.

Number of squares shaded	Number of flags
1	3
2	6
3	10
4	12
5	12
6	10
7	6
8	3
	Total 62

Discussion points

Some pupils will find it difficult to spot lines of symmetry away from the horizontal and vertical

It is important to highlight that some shapes are 'negative images' of others.

A MASS OF TEST PAPERS

A school finds that it is wasting a great deal of A4 paper because it throws out all exam papers and old worksheets. The pupils in the school decide to collect and sell them for recycling. They have found that they can sell 10 kg of paper for 13p.

In order to check how well they are doing, one class thinks it would be a good idea to make a scale next to which the paper could be piled so the success of the collection can be seen.

Design an accurate scale, marked for every 10 kg, to show the height of 100 kg of A4 paper.

Ideas

It is unlikely that you will have the scales to weigh 100 kg of paper, so you will have to weigh and measure a smaller amount of paper and use this information to construct your scale.

Development

You will need a supply of A4 paper to use in this investigation.

1 (a) Weigh out 1 kg of A4 paper.

  (b) Measure the height of the 1 kg of A4 paper.

  (c) You can now calculate the height of a 10 kg pile of A4 paper.

2 Now draw your scale. Mark off every 10 kg up to 100 kg. Show the measurements between each set of markings.

3 Could there be anything that affects the accuracy of your scale?

Extension

Find the thickness and mass of **one** sheet of A4 paper as accurately as possible.

From 'Hole numbers' and other practical investigations © Cambridge University Press 1992

A MASS OF TEST PAPERS – *NOTES*

National Curriculum attainment targets

AT1/4a, b, c   AT2/4a, b, c, e, 5d

Preknowledge

Experience of weighing and of measuring length

Skills to be developed

The levels of accuracy needed when weighing and measuring length
Use of simple scales

Equipment

Weighing scales   Rules   A4 paper

Solution

The pupils' answers may depend on the type of paper used, the 'newness' of the pile and whether it has had holes punched in it or not.

The following results are from using unpunched plain A4 paper at 80 g m^{-2}.

1, 2   1 kg measures   1.9 cm   2.0 cm
10 kg measures   19 cm   20 cm
100 kg measures   190 cm   200 cm

The scale will be like this:

kg	100	90	80	70	60	50	40	30	20	10	0
cm	200	180	160	140	120	100	80	60	40	20	0

3 Possible factors affecting accuracy may be punched holes, newness of paper, compression and the dampness of the paper.

Extension

The thickness of a sheet of paper is 0.1 mm and its mass is 5 g to 1 significant figure.

Discussion points

Other factors will also affect the accuracy of the final scale; for example, the type of paper and the effect of compression at the bottom of a high pile of paper.

It may be a good exercise for each group to count the number of sheets in their 1 kg pile, to extend the discussion on accuracy.

CHALLENGE

Many greetings cards use pop-up images to make them more interesting.
You are asked to design and make a pop-up card to send to a friend.

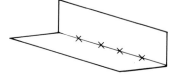

Ideas

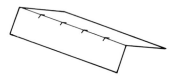

Here are some ideas to help.

Crossed folds show valley folds.

Folds drawn with a line through show hill folds.

To make a pop-up Christmas tree

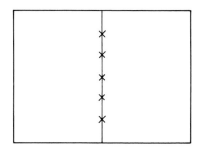

Get a sheet of paper 15 cm wide and 21 cm long, and fold it in half.

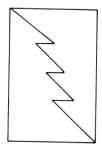

Draw half a Christmas tree on the folded paper. Make sure the tree starts at the top of the fold and the bottom of the tree is at the bottom outside corner of the paper.

Cut out the Christmas tree and colour both sides.

29

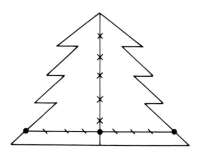

Open up the tree, draw a line 1 cm from the bottom, cut 1 cm up the central fold, then fold back the flaps. Next mark three dots as shown.

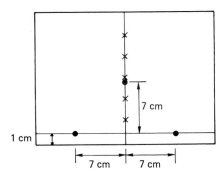

Fold a sheet of A4 paper in half and open it out again. Mark three points as shown.

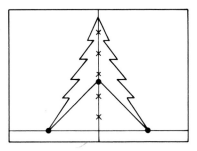

Glue under the flaps and stick the tree carefully onto the A4 paper, making sure that the dots on the paper match up with the dots on the tree. Allow the glue to dry. Now you can make the tree pop up.

30

To make a chair

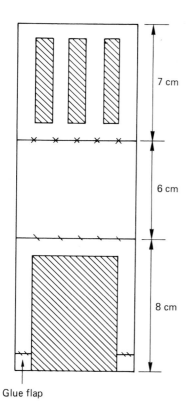

Cut out a rectangle 7 cm by 21 cm. Draw the chair as shown and cut out the shaded areas. Colour the chair and fold the paper according to the marks.

7 cm

6 cm

8 cm

Glue flap

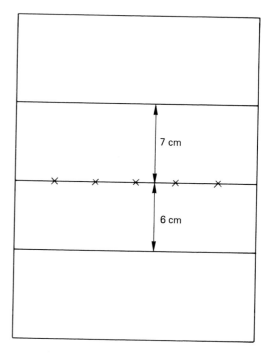

7 cm

6 cm

Fold a sheet of A4 paper in half and open it up again. Mark these lines, which will help you to position the chair.

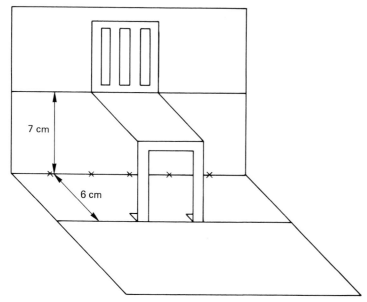

7 cm

6 cm

Glue the chair into place as shown. After the glue is dry, you can make the chair pop up.

National Curriculum attainment targets

AT1/4a   AT4/4a, 5a

Preknowledge

Ability to measure to the nearest millimetre
Spatial appreciation
Experience of commercial pop-up books and greetings cards

Skills to be developed

Simple mechanics
Following instructions and adapting them to different designs
Using two-dimensional and paper-folding techniques to represent
three-dimensional objects.

Equipment

Paper   Scissors   Good glue   Colours

Solution

Possible designs may incorporate:
a Valentine heart
an Easter chick with opening beak

Discussion points

Explain and demonstrate valley and hill folds.

This is an ideal opportunity for cross-curriculum activity.

Children should be encouraged to work together to make a joint book.

CHALLENGE

Gina has lots of books scattered around her room. Her parents are visiting at the weekend so she needs to make a temporary bookcase. She asks the builders who are altering a flat next to hers if she can borrow some bricks and planks of wood. She doesn't want to have spare bricks or planks of wood lying around her flat when she has finished so she needs to find a connection between the number of layers, planks and bricks used in the bookcase design.

This is a two-layer bookcase of the type Gina is planning to make. Eight bricks and three planks have been used.

Find the connection between the number of layers, planks and bricks used for bookcases made by Gina.

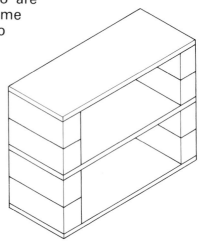

Ideas

You may find it helpful to make the bookcases out of Lego.

To simplify the problem, make a bookcase one layer high and then build it up one layer at a time.

Development

1 Make a bookcase one layer high. How many planks and bricks are used?

2 Make about six different larger bookcases. Keep a record of bricks and planks used. It would be sensible to write your findings in a table as this will make it easier to spot patterns. Remember, you are collecting information about the number of layers, number of bricks and number of planks.

3 Find the connection between the number of layers in the bookcase and the number of planks used.

4 Find the connection between the number of layers in the bookcase and the number of bricks used.

5 Can you find the connection between the number of planks and the number of bricks?

6 Using the connections you have found, predict how many planks and bricks would be needed to make a bookcase 10 layers high.

Extension

Design a different style of bookcase using bricks and planks. Write down any connections between the numbers of bricks, planks and layers.

33

From 'Hole numbers' and other practical investigations © Cambridge University Press 1992

National Curriculum attainment targets

AT1/4a, b, c, d   AT3/4a, b, 5b

Preknowledge

Ability to record results in a table
Experience of spotting connections between sets of numbers

Skills to be developed

Finding a simple start to a problem
Working systematically
Clear recording of results
Finding relationships and writing down expressions
Testing relationships found

Equipment

Lego

Solution

Challenge

Number of layers + 1 = number of planks
Number of layers × 4 = number of bricks
(Number of bricks ÷ 4) + 1 = number of planks

Development

1 2 planks and 4 bricks

2 The pupils devise their own bookcases and methods of recording. The following table should help:

Number of layers	Number of planks	Number of bricks
1	2	4
2	3	8
3	4	12
4	5	16
5	6	20
6	7	24
7	8	28
8	9	32

3 The number of planks (p) is one more than the number of layers (l).

$$p = l + 1$$

4 The number of bricks (b) is four times the number of layers.

$$b = 4l$$

5 $\quad 4(p - 1) = b$

6 10 layers, 40 bricks, 11 planks

Extension

The pupil's own bookcase design and connections. Possible changes could be: three bricks between shelves for taller books; using two planks for each shelf and a second set of bricks, for wider books

Discussion points

Pupils may need to be shown how to find connections in a table. If one set of numbers is going up in ones and its related set is going up in fours, then there is a 'multiply by 4' relationship.

Discuss the importance of testing to ensure the relationship is correct.

CHALLENGE

Here are two examples of single layered cuboids.

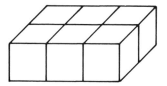 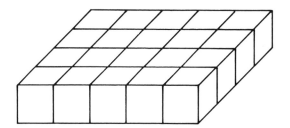

This is a 3 by 2 single layered cuboid. This is a 5 by 4 single layered cuboid.

How can you tell which single layered cuboids can be made up from

(a) double blocks, (b) triple blocks?

Ideas

Look first at the single layered cuboids you can make with double blocks.

Here is an ordered table of single layered cuboids.

~~1 by 1~~	(2 by 1)	3 by 1	4 by 1	5 by 1	6 by 1
	2 by 2	3 by 2	4 by 2	5 by 2	6 by 2
		3 by 3	4 by 3	5 by 3	6 by 3
			4 by 4	5 by 4	6 by 4
				5 by 5	6 by 5

Make some double blocks out of click-together cubes. See which single layered cuboids in the table can be made from these double blocks.

Development

1 Copy the table. Why don't you need to include the 1 by 2, 1 by 3 and 2 by 3 in your table?

2 It is clearly impossible to make a 1 by 1 single layered cuboid from a double block. Put a line through this in your table. You obviously can make a 2 by 1 single layered cuboid from a double block; put a ring around this in your table. Your table should look like this.

1 by 1	2 by 1	3 by 1	4 by 1	5 by 1	6 by 1
	2 by 2	3 by 2	4 by 2	5 by 2	6 by 2
		3 by 3	4 by 3	5 by 3	6 by 3
			4 by 4	5 by 4	6 by 4
				5 by 5	6 by 5

Work through the table in an organised way, crossing out all the single layered cuboids which can't be made from double blocks and putting a ring round those which can.

3 Find a rule which tells you which single layered cuboids can be made from double blocks.

4 Work in a similar way using a table to find a rule which tells you which single layered cuboids can be made from triple blocks.

Extension

Look at different sized and shaped blocks and try to find rules which tell you which cuboids can be made from them. The cuboids need not be single layered.

37

BUILDING BLOCKS – *NOTES*

National Curriculum attainment targets

AT1/4a, b, c, d   AT2/4a   AT3/4a   AT4/4a

Preknowledge

Simple understanding of multiples of 2 and 3
Understanding of the term 'cuboid'.

Skills to be developed

Simple packing skills
Simple ordered searching, taking account of both positive and negative
outcomes to help formulate a rule

Equipment

Unit cubes

Solution

1 By symmetry a 2 by 1 cuboid is the same as a 1 by 2 cuboid. Similarly
for the 1 by 3 and 2 by 3 cuboids

2

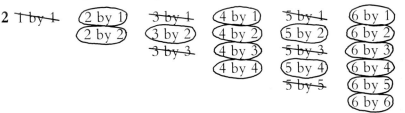

3 The single layered cuboids that can be made from double blocks are all
those where length × width gives an even number or if either side is
even. For example, a 4 by 3 cuboid can be made from double blocks
because 4 × 3 = 12 which is even; a 5 by 5 cuboid cannot be made
from double blocks because 5 × 5 = 25 which is odd.

4

1 by 1   2 by 1   (3 by 1)   4 by 1   5 by 1   (6 by 1)
            2 by 2   (3 by 2)   4 by 2   5 by 2   (6 by 2)
                       (3 by 3)   (4 by 3)   (5 by 3)   (6 by 3)
                                    4 by 4   5 by 4   (6 by 4)
                                               5 by 5   (6 by 5)
                                                          (6 by 6)

The single layered cuboids that can be made from triple blocks are all
those where length × width gives a multiple of 3 or if either side is a
multiple of 3.

Discussion points

The setting up of an ordered table, before starting the main question, is a
valuable technique.

Emphasise that 'discounted' information can be as valuable as 'retained'
information when formulating a rule.

38

CHALLENGE

How many different sized squares can be drawn on an 8 by 8 grid of dots? Here is an example.

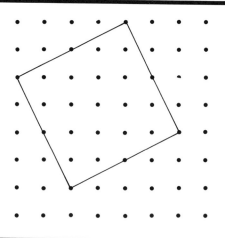

Ideas

It would be difficult to find all the different sized squares by working immediately on an 8 by 8 grid of dots. It is easier to look at a smaller size of grid to see what squares can be found. Start with a 3 by 3 grid (a 2 by 2 grid is too easy!) and then go on to larger grids.

Development

Ask your teacher for the worksheets.

1 It is possible to draw three different sized squares on a 3 by 3 grid of dots. Here is one of them.
Draw the other two on your worksheet. Make sure they are both different from the one here.

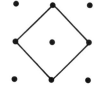

2 Now look at a larger grid. A 4 by 4 grid is the next size up. What is the maximum number of different sized squares that can be drawn on a 4 by 4 grid of dots? Draw them all on your worksheet.

3 Continue to increase the size of grid in an orderly way. Record the number of different sized squares that can be drawn on these grids in a table.

4 Use your table to help you to predict how many different sized squares can be drawn on an 8 by 8 grid of dots. Check your answer by drawing and ensure that all your squares are different. (Be careful!)

Extension

39

Can you extend the table further and predict any other hiccups in the pattern?

FINDING SQUARES – *NOTES*

National Curriculum attainment targets

AT1/5a, b, c   AT3/4a   AT4/4a, 5b

Preknowledge

Knowledge of what is meant by a square
Working out the area of a square
Experience of conducting a systematic search

Skills to be developed

Ability to recognise squares, including those away from the 'horizontal'
Understanding of the size of a square, that is that

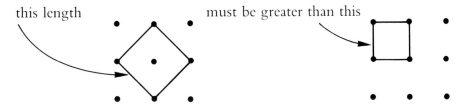

this length   must be greater than this

Predict a result by extending a table and testing for correctness of
prediction

Equipment

Squared spotty paper
Worksheets A and B (only for use with the development section)
Usual classroom equipment

Solution

1

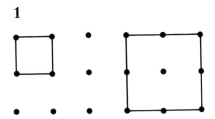

2 5 squares

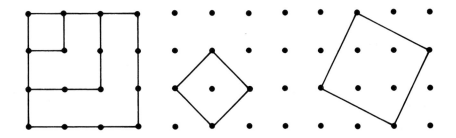

3

Size of grid	Number of different sized squares
2 by 2	1
3 by 3	3
4 by 4	5
5 by 5	8
6 by 6	11

4 The table above appears to have the pattern add 2, add 2, add 3, add 3. We can assume that we add 4 for a 7 by 7 grid, then add 4 for an 8 by 8 grid, and then add 5 and add 5.

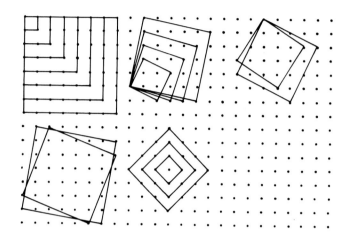

However, although there are 15 squares on a 7 by 7 grid, there are only 18 squares on an 8 by 8 grid because the two squares below are exactly the same size, both having a length of 5 units (Pythagorean '3, 4, 5' triangle).

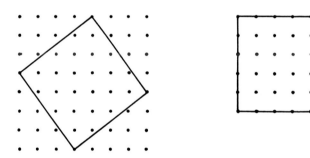

Extension

Further hiccups in the pattern will occur when Pythagorean triples are included.

Discussion points

Most children find it difficult to recognise differences in the lengths of the sides of some squares. To illustrate this a diagram like the one here may help to show the difference.

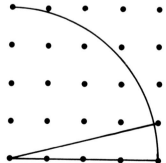

To draw a square on squared spotty paper it is useful to say 'go across 4 and down 1, then go down 4 and back 1' and so on.

Note the importance of a careful check of the answer.

MIND READING

CHALLENGE

Amaze your friends! Write the number 1 on a piece of paper and seal it in an envelope. Ask your friend to choose any number; add 5; multiply by 2; subtract 8; divide by 2; and subtract the number they first thought of. Astonishingly, their answer will be the same as the number in the envelope.

Ideas

To help solve this problem picture a bag of sweets as the number that the person has thought of. Adding 5 can be seen as adding 5 sweets, and multiplying by 2 means that you have twice as many bags and sweets.

Development

This diagram helps to explain why you always get the answer 1 whatever number you start with.

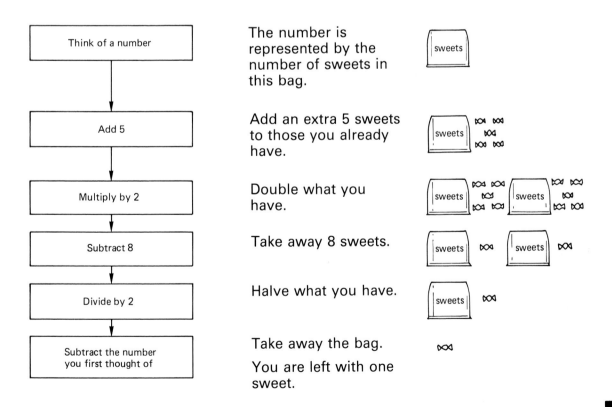

Think of a number	The number is represented by the number of sweets in this bag.	
Add 5	Add an extra 5 sweets to those you already have.	
Multiply by 2	Double what you have.	
Subtract 8	Take away 8 sweets.	
Divide by 2	Halve what you have.	
Subtract the number you first thought of	Take away the bag. You are left with one sweet.	

So, however many you first thought of (the number of sweets in the bag), you always end up with 1 (sweet).

From 'Hole numbers' and other practical investigations © Cambridge University Press 1992

MIND READING

1 Consider a simple situation where the result is 2 (sweets).

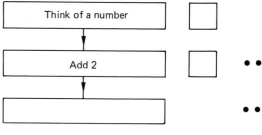

What instruction must go in the last box to get the answer 2?

Answer: 2 (sweets)

2 Here is a more complicated situation.

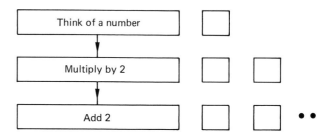

Because you have multiplied by 2 you have two bags of sweets to remove; dividing by 2 removes one bag of sweets.

(a) How can the other bag of sweets be removed?

(b) What is the outcome?

You are now ready to attempt some more difficult puzzles.

3 Complete this set of instructions so that the answer is always 3. Use the diagram to help you.

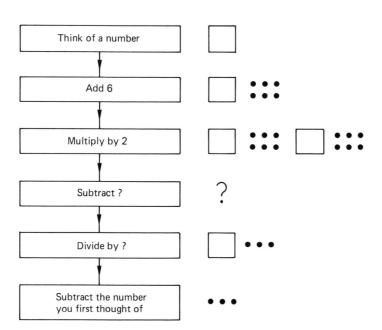

From *'Hole numbers' and other practical investigations* © Cambridge University Press 1992

4 Complete these instructions to give you an answer of 10. Use diagrams of bags of sweets if you wish.

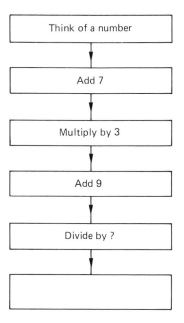

5 This is a more difficult set of instructions. Try to complete it so you will always end up with the number 7.

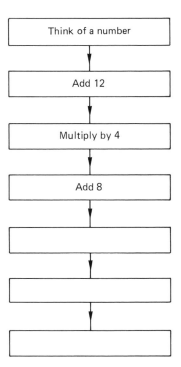

Work out your own puzzle and test it on your friends.

From *'Hole numbers' and other practical investigations* © Cambridge University Press 1992

MIND READING – *NOTES*

National Curriculum attainment targets

AT1/4b, c   AT3/4a, b

Preknowledge

Basic arithmetic
Knowledge of the idea of a symbol to represent an unknown number

Skills to be developed

Developing the idea of an unknown number
The ability to manipulate operations to achieve a desired result
Understanding of both additive and multiplicative inverses

Equipment

Usual classroom equipment

Solution

1 Subtract the number you first thought of

2 (a) Subtract the number you first thought of
   (b) 1

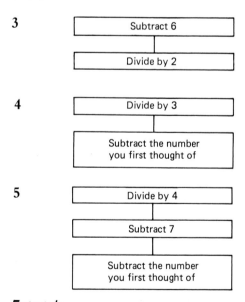

3

> Subtract 6
>
> Divide by 2

4

> Divide by 3
>
> Subtract the number you first thought of

5

> Divide by 4
>
> Subtract 7
>
> Subtract the number you first thought of

Extension

The pupil's own instructions

Discussion points

It may help some groups if an early question is demonstrated using a set of pencils.

Make sure that the idea of inverses is discussed fully.

CHALLENGE

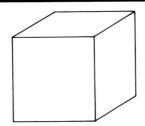

This is a drawing of a cube. It is a solid that has six square faces.

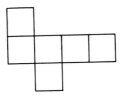

This shape is the net of a cube. If it is cut out and folded along the lines it makes a cube. (Copy the shape and try it out if you like.)

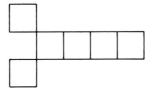

This is not the net of a cube because the squares on the left-hand side will fall off when it is cut out. The squares of a net of a cube must join together edge to edge.

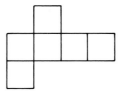

This net of a cube is the same as the first one. It is simply drawn a different way round.

Find all the different nets of a cube which can be made from six squares joined together. Use one of your nets to make a cube which has edges of length 5 cm.

Ideas

What is the greatest number of the six squares that can be joined together in a row to make a net of a cube? Find all the nets of a cube for this number of squares in a row, and then move on to shorter rows of squares.

From 'Hole numbers' and other practical investigations © Cambridge University Press 1992

Development

1 A row of six squares cannot be folded up to make a cube. Why not?

2 Can you make a net of a cube which contains a row of 5 squares?

3 Now look for nets which contain a row of 4 squares. Draw some rows of 4 squares and add a further two squares in different ways to make different nets.

4 Carry on working in an organised way to find all the other nets of a cube.

5 Check that all your nets are different and then write down the number of different nets you have found.

6 Choose one of the nets of a cube that you have found. Make an accurate drawing of the net onto card, remembering that the length of the sides will be 5 cm. You will have to add some fixing flaps like this

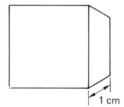

on the edges of some of the squares so the net can be glued to make a cube.

To do this you will need to think carefully about which edges will meet and put a flap on *one* of those edges.

Cut out your net, score carefully along the fold lines and glue it up to make a cube.

Extension

Not all nets of a cube have to be made from six squares.

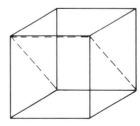

Imagine a cube which opens along the dotted line shown in the diagram.

1 Make a net of this cube.

2 Design some nets for other cubes which open in unusual ways. Make up a 5 cm by 5 cm by 5 cm cube out of card from the net you have designed.

From *'Hole numbers' and other practical investigations* © Cambridge University Press 1992

National Curriculum attainment targets

AT1/4a, b   AT4/4a

Preknowledge

Basic understanding of two and three dimensions
Familiarity with squares and cubes

Skills to be developed

Ability to conduct an organised search,
Recognise that solids can be made from more than one net
Ability to think in three dimensions whilst working in two dimensions
Constructing solids from nets

Equipment

Card   Scissors   Glue   Cube

Solution

1 A cube can only have four squares in a row. The two extra squares
   will just reinforce two of these four sides, leaving the top and bottom
   open.

2 A row of five squares will leave the box topless.

3

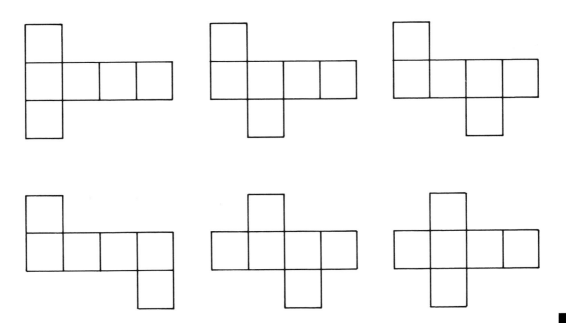

4

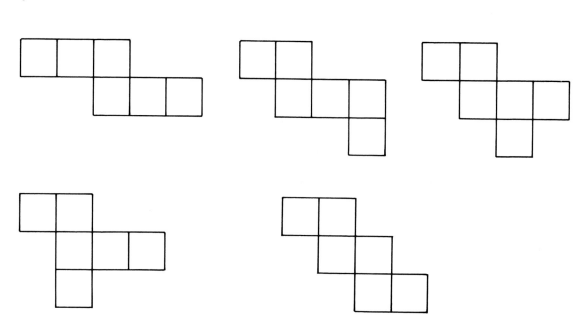

5 There are 11 possible different nets.

6 The pupil's own net.

Extension

1 A possible solution could be

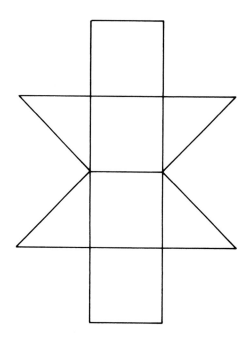

Discussion points

The idea of a systematic search should be emphasised.

CHALLENGE

You need 'The Hike' worksheet.

Two groups of walkers decide to hike from Stollywood to Finisham over some high moors, across rivers, over mountains and through thick woods. These obstacles are shown on the worksheet by boxes. The boxes have instructions which must be successfully completed before moving on. For example, if one group decides to go through 1a they must shake two dice and the total of the numbers must be 2 or 3. Each player starts at Stollywood. Players choose the route they are going to take: for example 1a, 2b, 3b, 4a. The first player tries to complete the instructions in a box. If the player is successful, they move their counter to the next circle; if unsuccessful, the counter stays where it is. The other player then has their turn. The winner is the first person to Finisham.
Work out which route is the best.

Ideas

First work out which is likely to be the best of each pair of boxes by experimenting with coins and dice. It will be easier if you work with somebody else.

Development

1 Throw two dice 100 times and record your results in a table.

Total score on dice	Tally	Total
2		
3		
⋮		
12		

2 (a) How many times did you get a total score of 7?
(b) How many times did you get a total score of 2 or 3?
(c) From your experiment which result do you think you are most likely to throw; a total score of 2 or 3, or a total score of 7?
(d) Is it best to go to box 1a or to box 1b?
3 Work through the other boxes by experimenting and decide which boxes are the best. State which route you find to be the best.
4 Compare your best route to that of other pupils.
5 Play the game several times with your partner. One player should go along the 'best' route and the other along the route which avoids the best route. Keep a record of who wins. Does the person using the best route always win? Explain clearly what you find.

50

From 'Hole numbers' and other practical investigations © Cambridge University Press 1992

THE HIKE – *NOTES*

National Curriculum attainment targets

AT1/5a, c   AT5/4b, d, 5d

Preknowledge

A basic knowledge of probability
Ability to perform simple experiments and record results clearly

Skills to be developed

Recognising that outcomes are not equally likely
Working out and comparing relative frequencies from experimental results

Equipment

Dice   Coins   Counters   Worksheet

Solution

The completion of the instructions in each box is related to the probability of the event occurring. An instruction with a high probability of happening is more likely to be completed before an instruction with a low probability. The probability of each of the boxes is as follows.

1a, $\frac{1}{12}$;   2a, $\frac{1}{2}$;   3a, $\frac{7}{12}$;   4a, $\frac{1}{6}$

1b, $\frac{1}{6}$;   2b, $\frac{1}{4}$;   3b, $\frac{1}{2}$;   4b, $\frac{3}{8}$

The route which is likely to be completed quickest is 1b–2a–3a–4b.

Discussion points

This exercise is a useful introduction to further work on attainment target 5/6c

The theoretical probabilities can then be compared with the experimental probabilities.

CHALLENGE

This is a square-based pyramid.

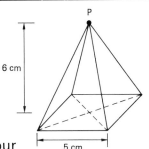

Design the net of this pyramid, and make a model from your design. The base must be a square with sides 5 cm long. The height of the pyramid from the centre of the square base to its vertex P must be 6 cm.

Ideas

First think about what the net of a pyramid will look like. Make a trial model out of paper and adjust your net if necessary before making your final model.

Development

1 Draw a sketch of the net of the pyramid and see which sides must be the same length. Check that your net makes a square-based pyramid.

2 Now draw your net accurately. Check that the corners of the base are right angles and make sure that the triangular faces are precisely drawn.

3 Add flaps to your net and then cut it out, score the fold lines and glue it to make a pyramid. Check that the dimensions of the pyramid are correct.

4 If any of the dimensions are wrong, explain which are wrong and why. Think about how the net folds to make the pyramid and what the dimensions should be.

   If your pyramid is correct, describe how you made sure that all the dimensions were right.

5 You may need to improve your net. It may be useful to draw accurate sections from your pyramid to help you find some missing lengths.

6 When you have redesigned your net, make it up into the pyramid. Again check that all the dimensions of the pyramid are correct. If your pyramid is now correct, show it to your teacher. If some of the measurements are still wrong, ask your teacher for help.

Extension

Make a cone which has a base diameter of 8 cm and a height of 6 cm.

From 'Hole numbers' and other practical investigations © Cambridge University Press 1992

THE PYRAMID – *NOTES*

National Curriculum attainment targets

AT1/5a, b, c   AT2/5c   AT3/5a, 5b

Preknowledge

Understanding of the words 'pyramid' and 'vertex'
Ability to use compasses and other drawing equipment
Ability to make three-dimensional models from nets

Skills to be developed

Ability to use the trial-and-improvement method in three-dimensional situations
Accuracy of construction of shapes in two dimensions to make three-dimensional models
Ability to visualise a plane within a solid

Equipment

Card   Scissors

Glue   Drawing instruments

Solution

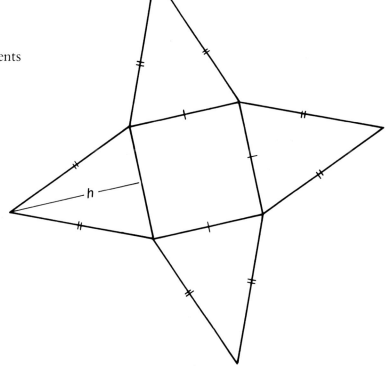

1 Pupils may design a different net although this is probably the simplest. Equal lengths are marked.

2 to 6 For the distance of P above the centre of the base to be 6 cm, we must use Pythagoras' theorem or an accurate drawing.

h = length of hypotenuse
$h^2 = 6^2 + 2.5^2$
$h = 6.5$ cm

An accurate net with the flaps might be:

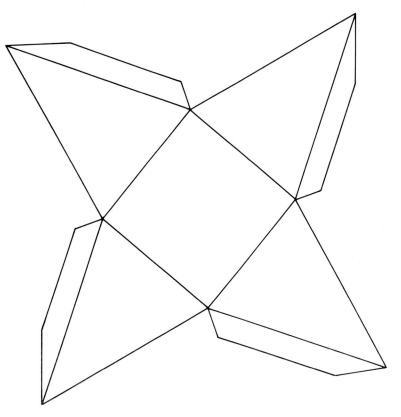

Extension

The net of the cone should be a sector of a circle, radius 7.2 cm to 2 s.f., and have an angle of 200° by calculation.

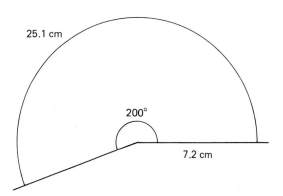

Discussion points

It is important to discuss the relationship between the height of the pyramid and the perpendicular height of a triangular face.

Discuss drawing sections from a three-dimensional figure to give a two-dimensional shape that can be worked on.

A useful way of checking the dimensions of a pupil's pyramid is to make 5 cm square and 6 cm high tube.

SQUARES IN SQUARES

CHALLENGE

Can you work out the total number of squares on a chessboard? There are many more than 64!

Ideas

You could try to draw all the possible squares on a chessboard, but this is very time-consuming and it would be easy to miss some squares. One way to start is to simplify the problem by looking at smaller 'chessboards'. 'Chessboards' have many different sized squares. It is easiest to count the smallest squares first and then look for the larger squares systematically.

Development

A 2 by 2 'chessboard' has four 'one squares':

and one 'two square':

making five squares in total.

1 How many squares are there altogether on a 3 by 3 'chessboard'? List the different sized squares separately; this makes it easier to spot any patterns.

    'one square'   . . .

    'two square'   . . .

    'three square' . . .
                       ———

    Total   ———

2 Using the method of question 1, find the total number of squares on a 4 by 4 'chessboard'.

3 The numbers in your tables (assuming they are right) have a special name. What is it?

4 Can you predict the table for a 5 by 5 'chessboard'?

5 Explain how the pattern develops for different sized 'chessboards'.

6 Now work out the total number of squares on a normal 8 by 8 chessboard.

Extension

55

How many rectangles are there on a chessboard? (Remember that squares are special rectangles.)

From 'Hole numbers' and other practical investigations © Cambridge University Press 1992

SQUARES IN SQUARES – *NOTES*

National Curriculum attainment targets

AT1/5a, b, c   AT3/4a, 5a

Preknowledge

Familiarity with square numbers
Organised searching

Skills to be developed

Searching for numerical patterns from spatial situations
Making and testing simple predictions
Recognising familiar number patterns in unfamiliar situations

Equipment

Squared paper

Solution

Challenge

There are 204 squares on a chessboard.

1	'one square'	9
	'two square'	4
	'three square'	1
	Total	14

2	'one square'	16
	'two square'	9
	'three square'	4
	'four square'	1
	Total	30

3 They are square numbers.

4 'one square'   25

'two square'   16

'three square'   9

'four square'   4

'five square'   1

Total   55

Pupils should check their answer with a drawing.

5 As the size of the 'chessboard' increases by one the next square number is added.

Number of squares in an n by n 'chessboard' $= \sum_{i=1}^{n} i^2$

$$= \tfrac{1}{6} n(n + 1)(2n + 1)$$

6 $1^2+2^2+3^2+4^2+5^2+6^2+7^2+8^2= 204$

Extension

The number of rectangles on a chessboard is 1296. This is the sum of the first eight cube numbers.

Discussion points

Discuss the use of a structured table to help to spot number patterns and the drawing of diagrams to verify predictions.

It is difficult to generalise in all situations. Extending a pattern may be the only alternative.

CHALLENGE

Write a report which shows how good pupils are at estimating
the size of angles.

Ideas

Draw different angles and ask other pupils to estimate the size of
each angle. Gather the information together and use statistical
methods (averages, range, spread, bar charts) to help you present
the information. Make suitable conclusions.

Development

1 (a) Estimate the size of this angle.

   (b) Ask all the pupils in your class to estimate the size of the
   angle. Keep a record of all their estimates.

2 (a) What was the largest estimate made for the angle?

   (b) What was the smallest estimate made for the angle?

   (c) What is the difference between the smallest estimate and the
   largest estimate? This is called the range of the estimates.

3 Calculate the mean estimate. To do this you add up all the
estimates and divide by the number of estimates.

4 (a) Put the estimates into suitable groups by drawing a table and
   using a tally chart.

Group	Tally	Frequency
0° – 10°		
11°		

   (b) Draw a frequency diagram (bar chart) for the estimates.

5 Here is another angle.

   Repeat questions 1 to 4 for this angle.

6 Measure the two angles with a protractor. Are the mean
estimates greater or less than the actual angles? By how
many degrees?

7 Which of the two angles were pupils best at estimating?
Explain your answer by looking at the means, ranges and
frequency diagrams.

58

From 'Hole numbers' and other practical investigations © Cambridge University Press 1992

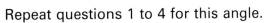

ANGLING – *NOTES*

National Curriculum attainment targets

AT1/5a, b   AT5/4c, 5b, d

Preknowledge

Understanding the concepts of mean and range
Measuring angles
Constructing bar charts

Skills to be developed

Collecting data and recording in an organised way
Grouping and displaying information appropriately
Using means and ranges in a real situation to interpret and compare results
Comparing calculated results with actual values

Equipment

Protractors   Graph paper

Solution

The size of the angles drawn on the page are 72° and 158°.

Discussion points

Make sure that there are no protractors available at the start of the exercise.

It would be wise to discuss the level of accuracy to which the mean value for the class should be rounded (to the nearest degree).

Be aware of estimates which are significantly different from the actual value and how these could be treated. When comparing the results for the estimates of large and small angles, the spread and the mean value are both important.

CHALLENGE

In an attempt to brighten up a classroom a pupil suggests that a display board could be tiled. Work out the total cost of doing this.

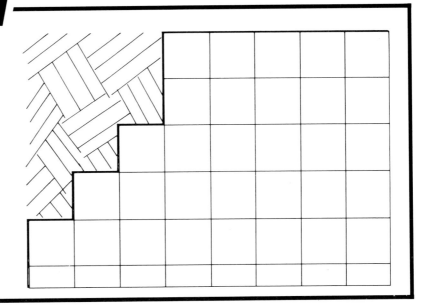

Ideas

First plan what you are going to do, what information you need to collect and what equipment you must buy.

Development

1 Measure the display board in your classroom which is to be tiled. Draw a sketch of the board and label all its measurements.

2 Find out the dimensions of the tiles which are to be used.

3 Decide how you are going to tile the board. Are you going to use just one type of tile, or more than one type?

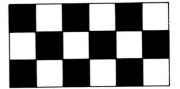

4 Work out how many tiles you need. You could draw an accurate scale drawing of the display board with the tiles marked. You could work out how many tiles fit along its length and how many along its width. From this you can work out how many tiles are needed. Make clear how you deal with part tiles. State the total number of tiles you need. List different types of tile separately as they may have different prices.

5 Work out the total cost of the tiles. You will have to find out the prices. Can they be bought separately or do they have to be bought in boxes of, for example, 20? Are the prices different for patterned and unpatterned tiles?

6 Find out the cost of all the other items you need. Some costs will have to be worked out whilst others can be found from a catalogue: make sure you show your workings. List the items needed and find the total cost.

60

From 'Hole numbers' and other practical investigations © Cambridge University Press 1992

TILING – *NOTES*

National Curriculum attainment targets

AT1/5a, b   AT2/4d, e, 5d

Preknowledge

Ability to use various types of measuring equipment, and to decide which
is the most appropriate
Ability to calculate area
Arithmetic skills (multiplication, division and money) on a calculator
Experience of rounding a calculator display
Experience of simple ratios

Skills to be developed

Using a wide range of mathematics in a real situation
Use and relevance of scale drawings
The importance of planning a task in advance and making adjustments as
the task is undertaken

Equipment

Tiles   Display board   Measuring equipment   A DIY catalogue

Discussion points

Thought must be given to the degree of accuracy required when
measuring.

Pupils need to be aware of sources from which information about sizes
and pieces of material can be obtained.

Pupils should be aware of the 'extra' cost of the labour to do the job.

CHALLENGE

A prime number is a number that can only be divided by itself and 1 to give a whole-number answer. So 13 is a prime number, but 9 is not because it can be divided by 1, 3 and 9 to give a whole-number answer.

A square number is a number which can be made by multiplying a whole number by itself. $3^2 = 3 \times 3 = 9$. So 9 is a square number.

Some prime numbers can be written as the sum of two square numbers. For example $13 = 4 + 9$. Since 2 squared $(2^2) = 4$ and 3 squared $(3^2) = 9$, it can be written as $13 = 2^2 + 3^2$

Try to find a rule which helps you to predict which prime numbers can be written as the sum of two square numbers and which cannot.

Ideas

Make lists of prime and square numbers. See which prime numbers can be made from square numbers and write these in a list. Make a separate list of those prime numbers that cannot be made from square numbers.

Development

1 Make a list of all the prime numbers which are less than 100 down the left-hand side of your paper.
2 Make a list of all the square numbers which are less than 100 down the right-hand side of your paper.
3 See which pairs of square numbers can be added together to make a prime number. It may be useful to think about what happens when you add:
   ● an even number to an even number;
   ● an even number to an odd number;
   ● an odd number to an even number;
   ● an odd number to an odd number;
   and to look at the nature of *most* of the prime numbers.

4 Make two lists – one of prime numbers which can be written as the sum of two square numbers and another of the prime numbers which cannot be written this way. Try to find what makes one list different from the other.

5 Check that your rule works for all prime numbers which are less than 100. Does it work for prime numbers greater than 100?

Extension

Look at your list of prime numbers which cannot be written as the sum of two square numbers. Can these be written as the sum of three or four square numbers? Are there any rules you can find to help you to predict these sums?

62

PRIMES AND SQUARES – *NOTES*

National Curriculum attainment targets

AT1/5a, c   AT3/5a

Preknowledge

Familiarity with prime and square numbers
Understanding of the term 'sum'
Experience of simple rules

Skills to be developed

Finding rules to give 'yes'/'no' predictions
Recognising that there can be relationships between seemingly unconnected sequences

Equipment   Calculators

Solution

1–4 Prime numbers from 1 to 100

Possible	Not possible	Possible	Not possible	Possible	Not possible
$2 = 1^2 + 1^2$	3	$29 = 2^2 + 5^2$	23	$61 = 5^2 + 6^2$	59
$5 = 1^2 + 2^2$	7	$37 = 1^2 + 6^2$	31	$73 = 3^2 + 8^2$	67
$13 = 2^2 + 3^2$	11	$41 = 4^2 + 5^2$	43	$89 = 5^2 + 8^2$	71
$17 = 1^2 + 4^2$	19	$53 = 2^2 + 7^2$	47	$97 = 4^2 + 9^2$	79
					83

Add 1 to the prime number and then divide it by 2. If the answer is even, the prime number cannot be expressed as the sum of two squares, otherwise the prime number can be expressed as the sum of two squares. This works for all prime numbers.

5   The rule works for prime numbers greater than 100 too. For example:

Prime numbers from 101 to 200		Prime numbers from 201 to 300		Prime numbers from 301 to 400	
Possible	Not possible	Possible	Not possible	Possible	Not possible
$101 = 1^2 + 10^2$	103	$229 = 2^2 + 15^2$	211	$313 = 12^2 + 13^2$	307
$109 = 3^2 + 10^2$	107	$233 = 8^2 + 13^2$	223	$317 = 11^2 + 14^2$	311
$113 = 7^2 + 8^2$	127	$241 = 4^2 + 15^2$	227	$337 = 9^2 + 16^2$	331
$137 = 4^2 + 11^2$	131	$257 = 1^2 + 16^2$	239	$349 = 5^2 + 18^2$	347
$149 = 7^2 + 10^2$	139	$269 = 10^2 + 13^2$	251	$353 = 8^2 + 17^2$	359
$157 = 6^2 + 11^2$	151	$277 = 9^2 + 14^2$	263	$373 = 7^2 + 18^2$	367
$173 = 2^2 + 13^2$	163	$281 = 5^2 + 16^2$	271	$389 = 10^2 + 17^2$	379
$181 = 9^2 + 10^2$	167	$293 = 2^2 + 17^2$	283	$397 = 6^2 + 19^2$	383
$193 = 7^2 + 12^2$	179				
$197 = 1^2 + 14^2$	191				
	199				

Discussion points

It is necessary to highlight the difference between a predictive rule and a formula. A predictive rule has limitations; for example, it cannot tell you which two square numbers add to make the prime.

CHALLENGE

Philippa Fisher decides to have a day's fishing at a large lake called Loadsafish. The lake owner guarantees that every time a line is cast into the lake a fish will be caught. The lake is stocked with equal numbers of six different kinds of fish. All the fish are equally likely to be caught. The six fish in the lake are: Eel   Perch   Trout   Carp   Bream   Roach

Show how many of each type of fish Philippa is likely to catch if she casts her line sixty times. Being a true angler, she throws the fish back into the lake after they have been caught.

Find how many times Philippa must cast her line in order to catch at least one of the different types of fish.

Ideas

It is clearly impossible to find Lake Loadsafish so in order to solve the problems we must *simulate* the situation by experimenting to find out what is to be the likely outcome. There are six different kinds of fish and the most obvious way to simulate the situation is by rolling a die because a die has six equally likely outcomes.

Development

1 (a) Give each of the different kinds of fish a number on the die. Roll the die sixty times and keep a record of your results in a table using tally marks.
   (b) Draw a bar chart to show the number of each type of fish caught in the sixty throws.
   (c) Compare your results with those of other pupils and write down anything you notice.

2 Use the same numbers to represent the fish for this question. You will need to experiment several times.
   (a) Make a list of the numbers from 1 to 6. Roll your die and cross off the numbers as you get them *and* at the same time keep a tally of the number of times you have rolled the die like this.

Fish caught (numbers on the die)	Tally	Total number of casts of the line
~~1 2 3 4 5 6~~	ЖЖ ЖЖ ЖЖ ΙΙ	17
~~1~~ 2 3 ~~4~~ 5 6	ЖЖ	

   (b) What do you notice about the number of times Philippa had to cast her line? Why do you think you had to experiment several times?
   (c) Calculate the mean number of times Philippa had to cast her line to catch one of each of the fish.
   (d) Compare your mean to that of other pupils in the class.

64

From *'Hole numbers' and other practical investigations* © Cambridge University Press 1992

FISHING – *NOTES*

National Curriculum attainment targets

AT1/5a, b, c   AT5/4b, c, d, 5d

Preknowledge

Ability to calculate and understand mean
Have experience of collecting, recording and displaying information

Skills to be developed

Developing a simple simulation technique
Analysing, interpreting and reporting simulated results
Understanding that there can be wide discrepancies between outcomes
when probabilities are involved

Equipment

Dice

Solution

Philippa should catch 12 of each fish if she casts the line 60 times. The
theoretical average number of casts is 14.7 to catch at least one of each
type of fish.

Discussion points

The display of the combined results should show a distribution similar to
this.

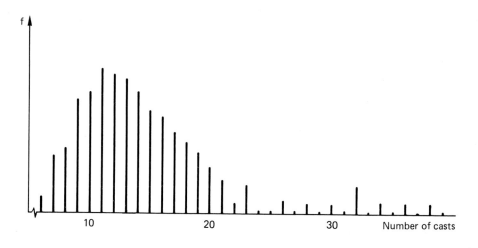

An answer closer to the theoretical solution can normally be obtained by
collecting together the results of each pupil's experiments.

CHALLENGE

Ann E. Mall is organising the children's pet competition at the Brighouse and District Agricultural Show. She has been given a trailer full of special sized continental bales of hay to make rectangular enclosures for the different types of animals.

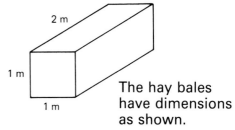

The hay bales have dimensions as shown.

With six hay bales she can make two different sizes of rectangular enclosure. One arrangement gives a rectangular enclosure of area 3 m².

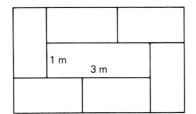

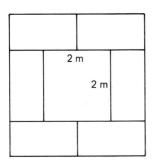

The other arrangement gives an area of 4 m² – just about right for showing the guinea pigs.

The bales must fit together neatly, so she cannot join them together

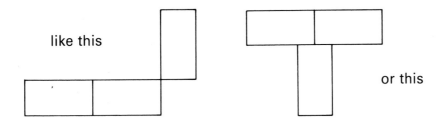

like this

or this

This arrangement cannot be used because it is not rectangular

and there must be some space inside the enclosure!

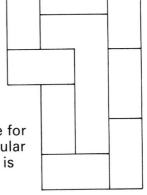

Ann has 50 bales available to make a rectangular enclosure for the dog obedience trials. How many different sized rectangular enclosures can she make using *all 50* of these bales? What is the largest area that can be enclosed?

66

From *'Hole numbers' and other practical investigations* © Cambridge University Press 1992

Ideas

You could use something like dominoes to represent the hay bales. Start with a small number of bales to make an enclosure. Increase the number of bales by one each time to make bigger enclosures.

Development

It is obviously impossible to make an enclosure from just one bale!

1 What is the smallest number of bales which can be used to make a rectangular enclosure? What is the area of this enclosure?

2 Work systematically and increase the number of bales by one each time. Find the number of different sized rectangular enclosures that can be made and the largest area that can be enclosed with different numbers of bales. Record your results in an organised table. (You will need at least eight entries in your table.)

3 Write down any patterns that you notice.

4 Extend your table without making the rectangular enclosures out of dominoes; then *check* your predictions by making the enclosures from the dominoes.

5 If you have found that your table is correct, find the number of different sized rectangular enclosures that can be made from the 50 bales and the largest area that can be enclosed. (Hint: you may wish to separate the odd from the even number of bales.) Explain clearly how you worked out the answers.

From *'Hole numbers' and other practical investigations* © Cambridge University Press 1992

THE AGRICULTURAL SHOW – *NOTES*

National Curriculum attainment targets

AT1/7a, b   AT3/5a, b, 7a   AT4/5d

Preknowledge

Must be able to calculate the area of rectangles
Understand square numbers

Skills to be developed

The use of a 'trial-and-improvement' method to maximise
Generalising from number patterns
Dealing with separate solutions (odd and even) to a single problem

Equipment

Dominoes   Squared paper

Solution

1 4 bales give an enclosure of 1 m^2

2

Number of bales (n)	Number of different sized enclosures (e)	Largest area in m^2 (a)
4	1	1
5	1	2
6	2	4
7	2	6
8	3	9
9	3	12
10	4	16
11	4	20
12	5	25
13	5	30
14	6	36
15	6	42
16	7	49
17	7	56
18	8	64
19	8	72
20	9	81
21	9	90

3 Splitting the table up into even numbers of bales and odd numbers of bales we get:

	Evens				Odds	
n	**e**	**a**		**n**	**e**	**a**
4	1	1		5	1	2
6	2	4		7	2	6
8	3	9		9	3	12
10	4	16		11	4	20
12	5	25		13	5	30
14	6	36		15	6	42
16	7	49		17	7	56
18	8	64		19	8	72
20	9	81		21	9	90

For even numbers of bales,

$$e = (n \div 2) - 1$$

$$a = e^2 \quad \text{(square numbers)}$$

$$a = [(n \div 2) - 1]^2$$

$$= \tfrac{1}{4} n^2 - n + 1$$

For odd numbers of bales,

$$e = (n - 3) \div 2$$

$$a = e\,(e + 1) \quad \text{(triangle numbers doubled)}$$

$$a = [(n - 3) \div 2] \times [(n - 3) \div 2 + 1]$$

$$= \tfrac{1}{4} n^2 - n + \tfrac{3}{4}$$

4 Pupil's own extension of the table and checking of prediction

5 For $n = 50$ bales, $e = 24$ and $a = 576$ m^2

Discussion points

It is true that bales of this size do exist!

The difference between the odd and even cases can usually be noticed in the repeat of the number in a column or the repeat of differences in a column.

There are three different styles of arrangement for the bales when joined together to make an enclosure.

For each number of bales there is a fixed inner perimeter. This limits the number of rectangular enclosures that can be made.

CHALLENGE

Andy Mann is a local builder who has been asked to build a wall between two classrooms at Teachem School, to stop pupils taking a short cut across the garden. The new wall is going to be 7.4 m long and about 1.3 m high. It will be two bricks thick. Andy wants to work out how many bricks he will need.

Ideas

Look at how a brick wall is built and measure the dimensions of a brick. Make sure you use the right dimensions when doing your calculations.

Development

1 What are the arrangement of the bricks in the wall? Sketch the arrangement. Why do you think they are arranged like this?

2 Make a list of measurements you will need in order to calculate the number of bricks in the wall. It may be useful to make a sketch and put your measurements on the sketch.

3 Look at the top layer of the wall. There are various ways in which the top of the wall can be finished off. Decide how you are going to arrange the top of your wall. Why is the top layer different from the other layers?

4 Collect the information you need and work out how many layers of bricks there will be. Think carefully about how the top layer should be taken into account.

5 Work out how many bricks you will need in each of the layers. State clearly how you are going to use part bricks.

6 Now work out the total number of bricks you will use to build the wall. Work out the height of your finished wall.

7 Check your answer is sensible. This can be done by actually counting the number of bricks in a square metre of wall and using this to give an approximate number.

Extension

Use a DIY catalogue to calculate the approximate cost of doing the job.

70

National Curriculum attainment targets

At1/5a, b   AT2/4c, d, e, 5d

Preknowledge

Experience of converting between metres and millimetres
Accurate use of a ruler

Skills to be developed

Appropriate rounding and approximation in a practical situation
Strengthening the understanding of dimensions – in particular working
out how many small lengths (in cm or mm) fit into a larger length in
metres

Equipment

Rule   Tape measure   Brick   A DIY catalogue

Solution

Most pupils will have different solutions depending on the arrangements
of the bricks and the thickness of mortar.

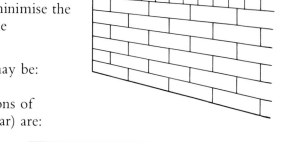

1 Most walls have the bricks in
an 'off-set' arrangement to minimise the
lines of weakness to make the
wall as strong as possible.

2, 3 A possible arrangement may be:

4, 5, 6 Assuming the dimensions of
a housebrick (including mortar) are:

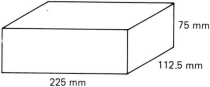

75 mm

112.5 mm

225 mm

then each double layer will need about 66 bricks (including a part of a
brick). There will be about 16 layers plus the top layer of nearly 100
bricks. A rough estimate using this type of brick will be about 1150 bricks.

Extension

Units of purchase must be considered carefully. You are unlikely to be
able to buy 1 kg of sand (a bag usually holds 38–50 kg). The mixture of
sand to cement is about 3 to 1. 100 bricks would use about 30 kg of cement.

Discussion points

Before starting the investigation, it is worthwhile to talk about the
orientation of a brick when used in a wall.
Consider the dimensions of a brick in the ratio of 2:3:6 when mortar is
taken into account.
Ensure that the thickness of mortar is considered.

HOLE NUMBERS

Look at a display board in your classroom which is full of staple or pin holes. Work out the approximate number of holes in the board.

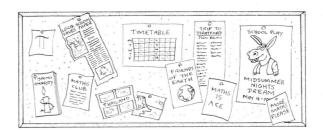

Ideas

It would take a very long time to count all the holes in the whole board! It is possible, however, to count the holes in part of the board (a sample) and use this to estimate the number of holes in the whole board.

Development

1 Guess the number of holes in the board. Write down your guess.

2 Make a 10 cm by 10 cm square hole in a sheet of paper. This is your 'sampler'. Place your sampler over any part of the board. Count the number of holes within the sampler and use this information to estimate the number of holes in the board:

(a) work out the total area of the board and of your sampler in m^2;

(b) divide the area of the board by the area of the sampler;

(c) multiply the number of holes in the sampler by the number of times the sampler fits onto the board to give an approximate number of holes in the board. Show all your working.

3 Is your estimate greater or less than your original guess? By how much greater or less?

4 Compare your answer with those of other pupils. Why might your answers vary?

5 Your estimated number of holes should be improved by taking more samples. Take more samples from different parts of the board. Work out the mean number of holes for each sample and use this to calculate the estimated number of holes in the board. Compare your answers and comment on your results.

Extension

Some areas of the board may have more holes than others. By taking this and other points into account, calculate an improved estimate of the number of holes in the board.

72

HOLE NUMBERS – *NOTES*

National Curriculum attainment targets

AT1/7a, b   AT5/7a

Preknowledge

Calculating a mean
Measuring and calculating areas
Understanding and using proportionality

Skills to be developed

Using a sample, estimate a population
Looking at how sampling technique can be bettered to obtain an improved result

Equipment

A classroom display board with many staple or pin holes
Tape measures and rulers

Solution

Individual pupils will have varying answers but they should tend towards the mean solution for the whole group.

Extension

Pupils may suggest taking corner, side and middle samples and to work on them separately.

Discussion points

Discuss what size of sampler is best; how the placement of the sampler over the display board can be randomised; and the number of samples taken when calculating a mean sample number.

The accuracy of the answer will vary significantly depending on the location of the sampler.

BILL E. BADGER FOR PRESIDENT

CHALLENGE

Bill Ewart Badger is running for President of the United States of America. As part of his campaign he wishes to give away badges which say 'Better Badger Than Bush'. His cousin is the boss of Brock Badge Inc, which makes badges out of metal discs 3 cm diameter. The discs are stamped out of rectangular sheets which can be bought in three sizes:

(a) 9 cm by 13 cm
(b) 11 cm by 14 cm
(c) 18 cm by 16 cm

Find the maximum number of discs which can be stamped out from each of the sheets.

Ideas

To do this you must think of the different ways in which the discs can be arranged on each sheet. For each sheet, use the arrangement which gives the most discs.

Development

The circles can be arranged inside a rectangle in rows, like this.

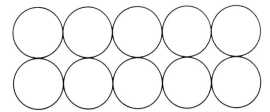

1 Draw any other possible regular arrangements you can find.

2 Draw 9 cm by 13 cm rectangles accurately and carefully. Make sure the corners are right angles. Inside, draw 3 cm diameter circles to show how the discs should be stamped out of the sheet. (Make sure your circles do not overlap.)

3 Which arrangement is best for a 9 cm by 13 cm rectangle?

4 Draw rectangles to represent the other two sizes of sheets and draw the arrangements of how the discs can be stamped out from these sheets. State clearly which arrangement is the best for each sheet.

Extension

Which is the best size of sheet to use in terms of producing the least waste?

74

From 'Hole numbers' and other practical investigations © Cambridge University Press 1992

National Curriculum attainment targets

AT1/6a,b   AT4/4a, 5d

Preknowledge

Ability to maximise results by trial and improvement

Skills to be developed

An appreciation of the way in which circles can be arranged

Equipment

Squared paper   Compasses
Old 10p coins will give circles of about 3 cm when drawn around

Solution

1

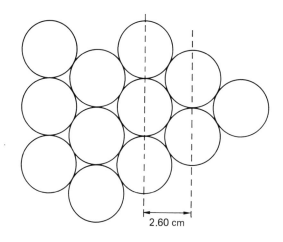

2.60 cm

2, 3 The optimum arrangement for a 13 cm by 9 cm rectangle gives 12 discs, although other arrangements of fewer discs are possible.

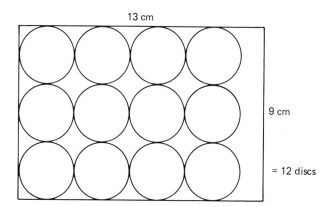

13 cm

9 cm

= 12 discs

4 This is the optimum arrangement for a 14 cm by 11 cm rectangle, which gives 16 discs.

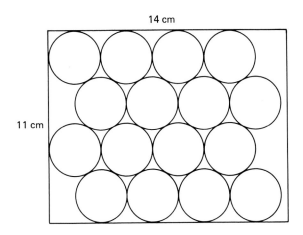

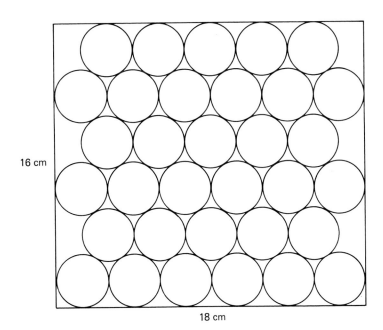

The optimum arrangement for an 18 cm by 16 cm rectangle gives 33 discs.

Extension

Wastage: (a) 27.5%; (b) 26.6%; (c) 19.0%.

Discussion points

Encourage pupils to notice that by having an offset row, it may be possible to fit in an extra row.

The importance of an accurate drawing should be emphasised.

CHALLENGE

This is a game for two players using an 8 by 8 grid of dots. The players take it in turns to mark a dot with a cross (×) or circle (○). Player 1 should use × and player 2 should use ○. The winning player is the person who first makes a row of four of their signs.

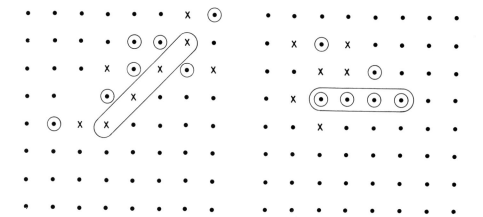

In this game player 1 has made a row of 4 crosses, and is the winner.

In this game player 2 has made a row of 4 noughts, and has won.

Can you find a way of beating everybody you play? Write a clear report of how your winning method works.

Ideas

Play the game a few times with a partner on the worksheet so that you can see how the game works. Write down anything you notice as you play the game.

Try to simplify the game. One way is to look at the starting positions.

Development

There are two starting positions for the game. One position is: ×   ○

1 (a) Why would the second player put a '○' next to the opening '×' and not elsewhere?
   (b) Explain why there are only two different sensible starting positions.
   (c) What is the other starting position?
2 Play the game with '× ○' as the opening and with the first player '×' to go next. Write down anything further that you find about how to win from this position.
3 Describe the winning strategy from the position '× ○'. Diagrams will help.
4 Now play the game from the other starting position and again write down the winning strategy using diagrams.

From 'Hole numbers' and other practical investigations © Cambridge University Press 1992

FOUR IN A ROW – *NOTES*

National Curriculum attainment target

AT1/7b

Preknowledge

Ability to play simple games of strategy such as 'noughts and crosses'
Recognising reflection and rotation of positions in a game

Skills to be developed

Ability to identify key features of a game strategy
Ability to consider all different options and to use logical reasoning to reject some options and accept others
Ability to describe strategies clearly

Equipment

Worksheet

Solution

The pupils may spot the following:
- There are only two sensible starting positions.
- Try to get three in a row with two free ends.
- You must try to block one side of two in a row with free ends, otherwise three in a row can easily be made.

1 (a) Otherwise the first player can easily create a winning position.

    (b) All other openings are reflections of others.

    (c)   ×
                 ○

2, 3 This is one possible solution, perhaps the easiest.

× ○
  ×
       Player 1 gets two in a row and ensures that the next nought which must block the line will not be next to the other ○.

× ○
  ×
    ○
       So player 2 puts a ○ at one end of the line of ×'s.

× ○
× ×
    ○
       Player 1 makes an 'L' shape. This gives two free 'two lines' which must be blocked by player 2 to prevent player 1 from getting a free three line of ×'s: obviously they can't.

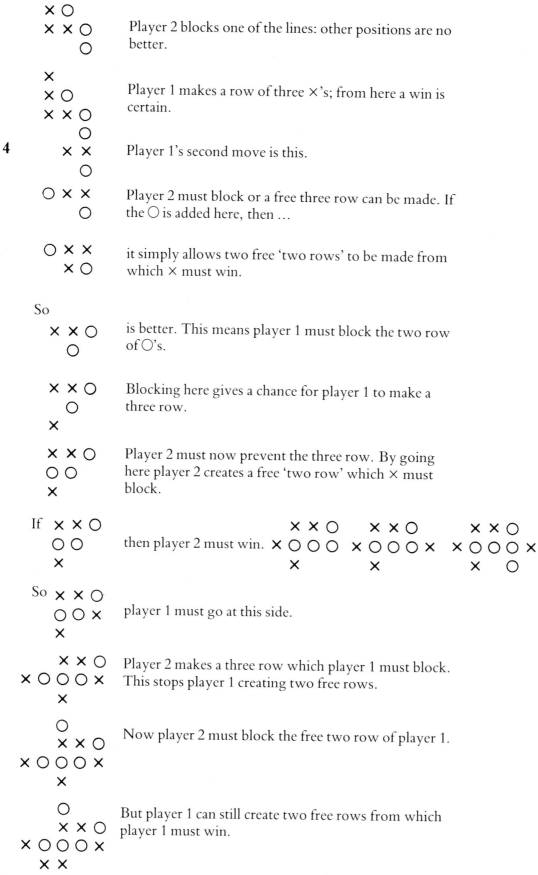

Player 2 blocks one of the lines: other positions are no better.

Player 1 makes a row of three ×'s; from here a win is certain.

4 Player 1's second move is this.

Player 2 must block or a free three row can be made. If the ○ is added here, then …

it simply allows two free 'two rows' to be made from which × must win.

So

is better. This means player 1 must block the two row of ○'s.

Blocking here gives a chance for player 1 to make a three row.

Player 2 must now prevent the three row. By going here player 2 creates a free 'two row' which × must block.

If

then player 2 must win.

So

player 1 must go at this side.

Player 2 makes a three row which player 1 must block. This stops player 1 creating two free rows.

Now player 2 must block the free two row of player 1.

But player 1 can still create two free rows from which player 1 must win.

Discussion points

The game brings out the importance of diagrams to illustrate the optimum strategies.

It is important to realise that complex situations may have only a few alternatives.

CHALLENGE

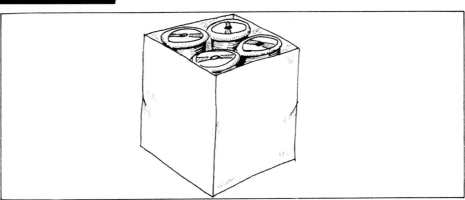

Design a cuboid box, without a top, which will hold twelve cotton reels.

You don't want to squeeze the reels into the box but you don't want them to slide about too much. You want to use as little card as possible so try to find the size of box which uses the least amount of card.

Ideas

First you will need to find out the dimensions of a cotton reel. The cotton reels can be arranged in many different ways. You need to arrange the reels in such a way that the least card is used for the box. Choose the simplest arrangement of cotton reels and then more complex arrangements.

Development

1 Measure a cotton reel and write down the dimensions.

2 (a) Draw a sketch of the net for a cuboid box which should hold the twelve reels arranged in a single row. Remember that the box does not need a lid. Ignore the flaps and fixing points. Label the measurements on your net.

(b) Work out the area of the net of this cuboid. This will be the area of card needed to make the cuboid box.

(c) Look at other arrangements of 12 cotton reels in a single row. Draw the net of the box which was the least amount of card.

3 Look at different ways of arranging the cotton reels. Draw and label the nets for each arrangement. Work out the area of card that would be used to make the boxes.
Which arrangement uses the least card?

4 Check that your box design is correct. Make up your best design into a box by first adding the flaps and fixing points. Check that it holds the twelve cotton reels.

80

A REEL PROBLEM – *NOTES*

National Curriculum attainment targets

AT1/7a   AT4/6a, 7d

Preknowledge

A simple understanding of area
Ability to measure to the nearest millimetre
Experience of constructing three-dimensional models from nets
Basic understanding of packing solids

Skills to be developed

Optimising through trial and improvement
Careful construction of three-dimensional models
Calculating the area of nets

Equipment

Cotton reels (12)   Card   Scissors   Strong glue

Solution

1 These solutions are based on reels which, within the limits of
measurement, have height 3.5 cm and diameter 3.3 cm.

2 There are two basic arrangements of 12 cotton reels in a single row. The
box which uses least card will have one of its largest faces open.
Minimum area of card 437.58 cm^2

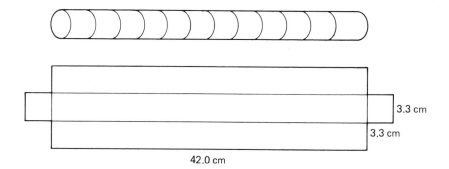

Minimum area of card 423.06 cm^2

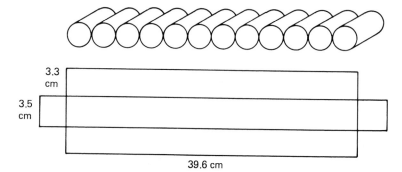

3 $2 \times 6 \times 1$

    length = $3.3 \times 6 = 19.8$ cm
    width = $3.3 \times 2 = 6.6$ cm
    height = 3.5 cm
      area = 315.48 cm^2

$4 \times 3 \times 1$

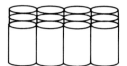

    length = 13.2 cm
    width = 9.9 cm
    height = 3.5 cm
      area = 292.38 cm^2

$3 \times 2 \times 2$

    length = 9.9 cm
    width = 7 cm
    height = 6.6 cm
      area = 292.38 cm^2

The two best boxes are:

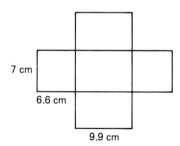
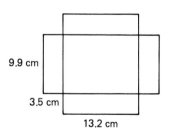

4 The pupil's own construction

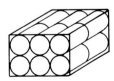
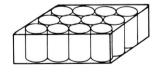

Discussion points

In how many ways can the cotton reels be arranged?
Which arrangement would be best from a manufacturer's point of view?

PROMOTION PACK

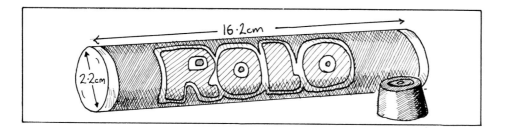

Rolos are normally sold in a packet 16.2 cm long and 2.2 cm in diameter.

W. H. Schmidt are organising a special Christmas promotion and have decided to sell packets of Rolos in individual boxes. Each cuboid box must just be big enough to hold one Rolo packet.

They have asked you to design and make a box. The box should be folded and glued from a single shape of card. It must have an opening face so that you can get out the packet of Rolos.

Explain carefully what you are doing and draw a plan to show how you have designed the box.

SQUARES

This 1 by 1 black square is surrounded by 8 other white squares.

1 How many white squares would be needed to surround this 2 by 2 black square?

2 How many white squares would be needed to surround different sized black squares?

3 Work out how many white squares are needed to surround a 78 by 78 square of black tiles. Explain your answer.

From 'Hole numbers' and other practical investigations © Cambridge University Press 1992

A landscape gardener has been asked to draw up plans for a grass and tree area behind a new row of shops which has just been built in Brighouse. The area is to be called Brighouse Copse.

Here is a sketch of the area:

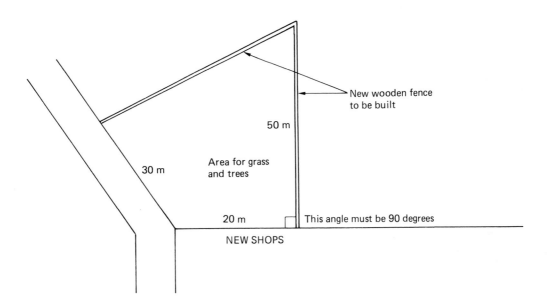

On your worksheet the pathway and shops have been drawn.

1 Using a scale of 1 cm to 2 m, make an accurate drawing of the position of the fences. One of the fences is 50 m long. Work out the length of the other and write its length on the worksheet.

2 Twelve trees are to be planted within the copse: 4 oak, 4 spruce and 4 cherry trees. The positioning of the trees is important. They have to be planted so that when they are fully grown they do not grow too close to the building, the path, the fence or each other. The trees must be planted at least 3 m away from the fences and at least 4 m away from the path.

Draw a boundary alongside the fences and the path to show the area in which the trees *should not* be planted.

This table gives some information about the trees.

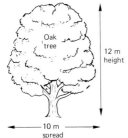

	Height	Spread
Oak trees	12 m	10 m
Spruce trees	20 m	4 m
Cherry trees	6 m	6 m

Trees cannot be planted within half their own height of any buildings.

Using the information, show where the trees should be planted. Make sure their positions fit all the necessary conditions. Write down any assumptions you make.

84

From *'Hole numbers' and other practical investigations* © Cambridge University Press 1992

WILLIE B. CONNED

Willie has to buy a secondhand car to go to work. For reliability it must be no more than 4 years old. Using your local newspaper as a source of information produce a report which details the price he could expect to pay.

MATCHSTICKS

This arrangement of matchsticks forms four squares.

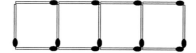

This arrangement forms fifteen squares.

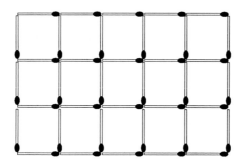

Investigate.

Promotion pack

	Indicators of general skills		Specific skills (AT1)
AT2/3e	Use the units cm and/or mm correctly. Accurate measurement to 2 mm	AT1/3d	Make a box, however crude, which holds a packet of Rolos. Make predictions to see where the flaps should go and test during construction
AT4/3a	Recognise that a three-dimensional figure is needed.		
AT4/4a	Use the terms 'parallel', 'perpendicular', 'face', 'edge' and 'vertex'. Construct shapes accurately: for example rectangles for net of cuboid. Construct a box in the shape of a prism.	AT1/4a	Draw a net and make a box which will hold together and
		AT1/4c	Accommodate a packet of Rolos.
AT4/6a	Make sure angles are drawn accurately.	AT1/5a	Make a box which snugly holds a packet of Rolos and/or state improvements necessary and/or improve box.
AT2/6g	A careful sketch of finished box with lengths in appropriate proportions.	AT1/6a	Evidence of different designs considered with reasoning, for example to minimise waste.

Squares

	Indicators of general skills		Specific skills (AT1)
AT3/3a	Recognising how the pattern continues. The pupil is able to continue the pattern 8, 12, 16, ...	AT1/3d	Drawing further diagrams, correctly counting white squares. Checking the results. Predicting the next number of white tiles and checking by use of a diagram.
AT3/4a	Describe how the pattern is developing: 'As the size of the black square is increased by 1 the number of white tiles increases by 4 because ...'	AT1/4a	Evidence of recording and tabulating results in an orderly manner from diagrams indicates a good level of planning.
AT3/4b	Recognise links between the size of the black square and the number of white tiles by example or machine chain $b \rightarrow \boxed{\times 4} \rightarrow \boxed{+ 4} \rightarrow w$	AT1/4c*	This will come from teacher-presented questions, e.g. 'How many white tiles would be needed to surround a 10 by 10 arrangement?' and a pupil check by drawing.

AT3/5a	To work out the number of white tiles you multiply by 4 for the four sides and add 4 for the corners.	AT1/5a	There is probably insufficient in the question to confirm a pupil's ability at this level.
AT3/5b	Using specific algebraic techniques $b \times 4 + 4 = w$ where $b = ...$ and $w = ...$	AT1/5c	Pupil makes own predictions and checks by drawing.

Brighouse Copse

	Indicators of general skills		Specific skills (AT1)
AT2/3e	Correctly state units for any line measured. Accurately measure any line to within 2 mm and accurately construct right angle to within 2 degrees.	AT1/3a	Check to see that the enclosure is a reasonable size and shape, for example, the unknown length should be a little more than 50 m by comparing sides.
AT3/4b AT4/4a	State or show that a cherry tree is 3 m, an oak tree 6 m and a spruce tree is 10 m away from building. State or recognise that the borders to the fence, path and building are lines parallel to those already drawn. Construct the enclosure using the given information.	AT1/4a AT1/4c	Show where trees cannot be planted State why a certain tree cannot be planted in a certain place.
AT2/5e AT4/5b	Accurately use the scale 1 cm to 2 m. Construct parallel lines accurately.	AT1/5a	Ensure that the trees are not too close to the building or each other. Ensure that the pupils have made sensible assumptions about the layout of the trees.
AT4/6a	Recognise and use the fact that a plan view of a tree will approach a circle, where the diameter of the circle equals the spread of the tree.	AT1/6a AT1/6c	Look for a change of layout or new plan for evidence of trial and improvement and/or cut-out circles that can be moved around. Ensure that the trees are sensibly spread, fit all requirements and are labelled. Any assumptions should be stated.

Willie B. Conned

	Indicators of general skills		Specific skills (AT1)
AT5/3a	Extract prices and age/year of car from source material.	AT1/3d	Check that the prices collected are within a sensible range.
AT5/3b	Construct simple car/price bar chart. Construct simple pictogram.		Predict that in general the price of cars falls as the age increases.
AT5/4b	Determine the number of cars available. Group the information according to price, type or age of car and determine the number of cars in each group. Construct a bar-line graph for the age/number of cars. Construct a frequency diagram for price of cars, labelling the price axis directly.	AT1/4a AT1/4c*	Evidence that the pupil has been selective about the data collected. Pupils respond to teacher's statements: 'two-year-old Ford Fiestas cost more than £3000' by using specific examples.
AT5/4c	Correctly calculate the mean and range of the prices.		
AT5/5b	Tabulate the information in an ordered way and draw valid conclusions. Classify the information and create frequency tables.	AT1/5a AT1/5c	Evidence of selecting data to make the task more manageable, for example, looking only at 1300cc cars. Pupils make statements such as all two-year-old Ford Fiestas cost more than £2500.
AT5/5c	Construct appropriate pie charts. Construct a frequency diagram of price against frequency with the price axis labelled continuously.		
AT5/6a	Determine criteria, group information and analyse the results. Design a questionnaire to gain information about the price and type of car to buy.	AT1/6c	Pupils draw clear conclusions, with supporting evidence, for example, more expensive cars depreciate at a quicker rate than less expensive cars.
AT5/6b	Construct a scatter graph showing the cost against age of comparable cars. Construct a two-way table in the form age of car against type of car, showing average price.		
AT5/7a	Find the mean, median, mode and range and compare results. Draw a line of best fit on the scatter graphs constructed.	AT1/7a	Make reasoned judgements about information within a category and treat exceptional cases sensibly.

Matchsticks

	Indicators of general skills		Specific skills (AT1)
AT3/3d	Extend a single sequence, for example a single row of squares 4, 7, 10, ...	AT1/3d	Draw further diagrams and correctly count matchsticks. Predict further matchsticks and check by drawing.
AT3/4a	Describe how the pattern is developing: 'as the length for a 2-wide array increases by 1, the number of matchsticks increases by 5'.	AT1/4a AT1/4c*	Evidence of recording and tabulating from diagrams with simple starting points in an orderly manner. This will come from teacher-presented question: 'How many matchsticks would be needed if your arrangement was 12 long?'
AT3/5a	Explain *how* the pattern is developing, possibly using diagrams.	AT1/5a AT1/5c	Work methodically through a 1 wide then 2 wide ... arrangement. Predict the number of matchsticks needed for a long arrangement and check by drawing.
AT3/6a	Generate and explain sequences in many or more different situations, for example the growth of square arrangements 4, 12, 24, ...	AT1/6c	Make a generalisation of the form 'length of the arrangement times 5 add 2 gives the number of matches' and test using diagrams and explain why the generalisation works.
AT3/7a	Write any rules and generalisations obtained in symbolic form.	AT1/7a AT1/7b	Attempt to draw together previous obtained rules into a single generalisation. Explain why the more complex generalisation works.

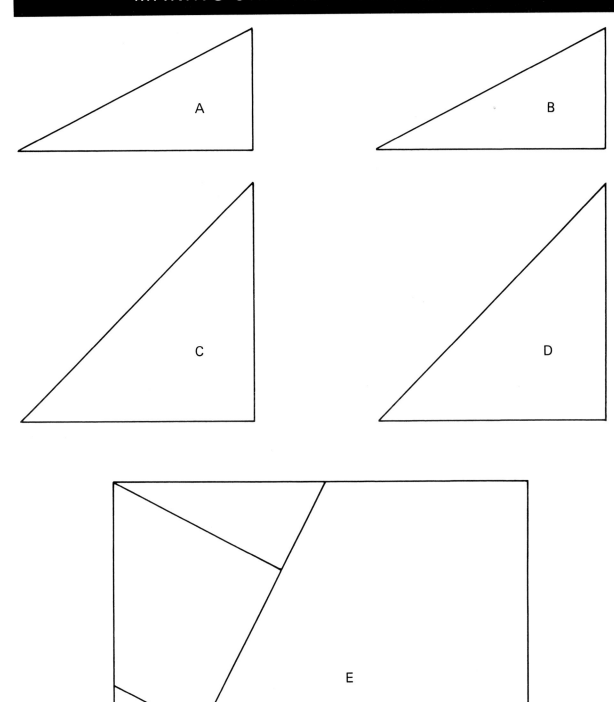

FINDING SQUARES – WORKSHEET A

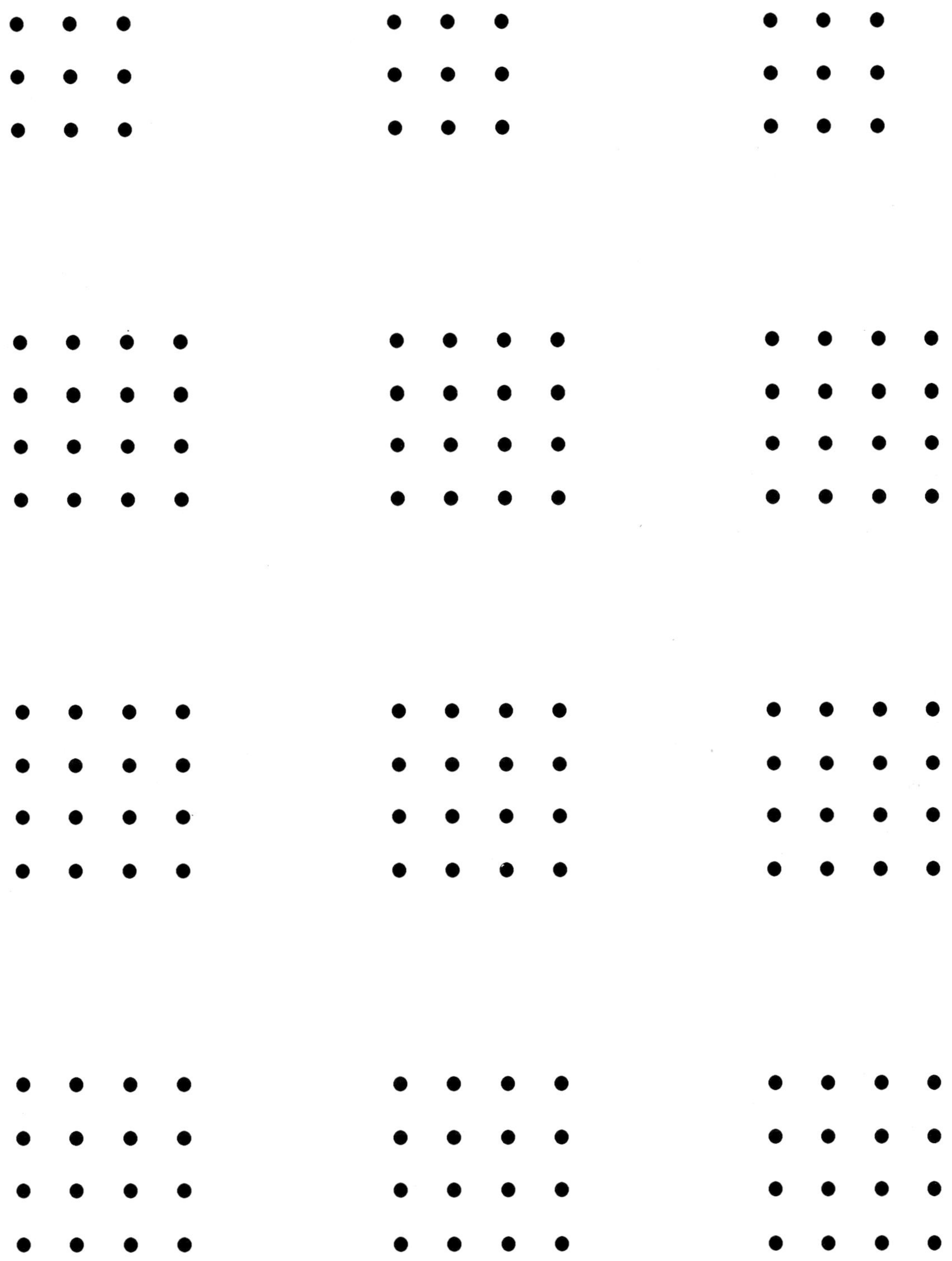

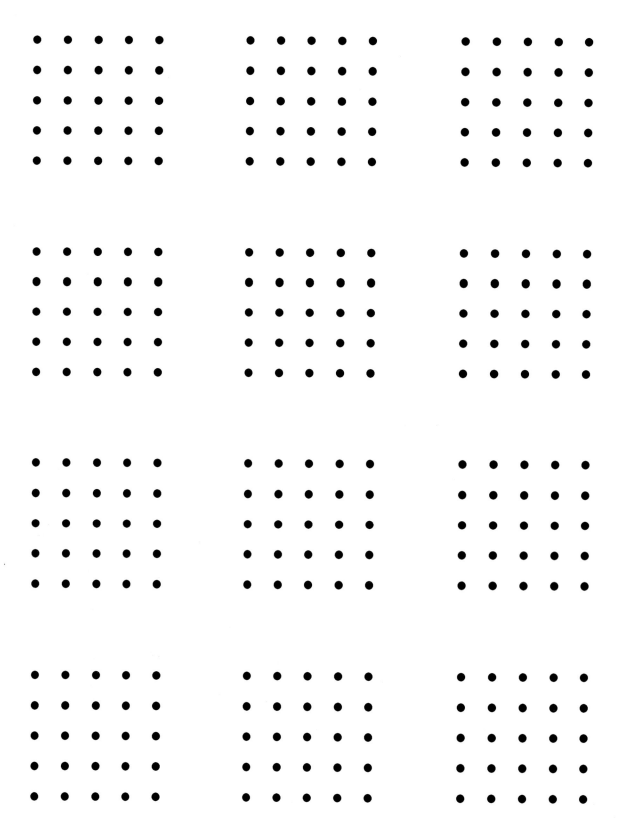

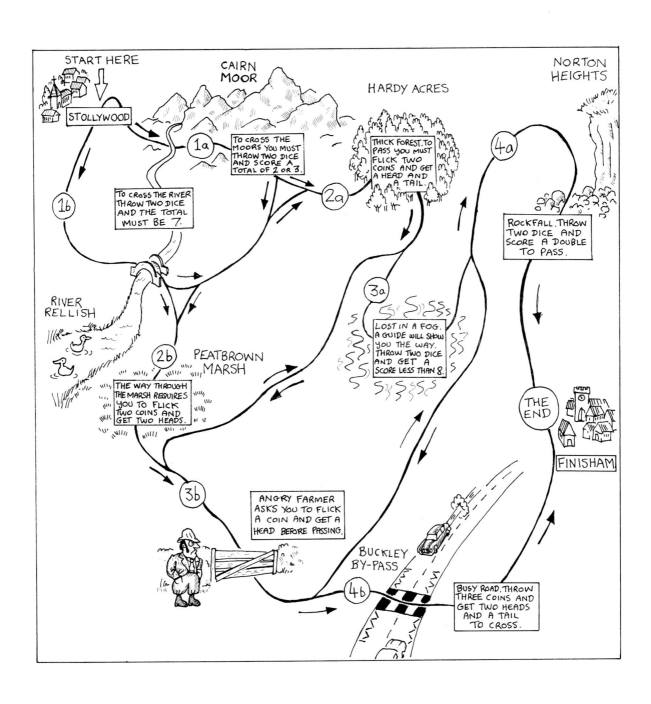

Scale

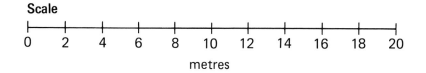

metres

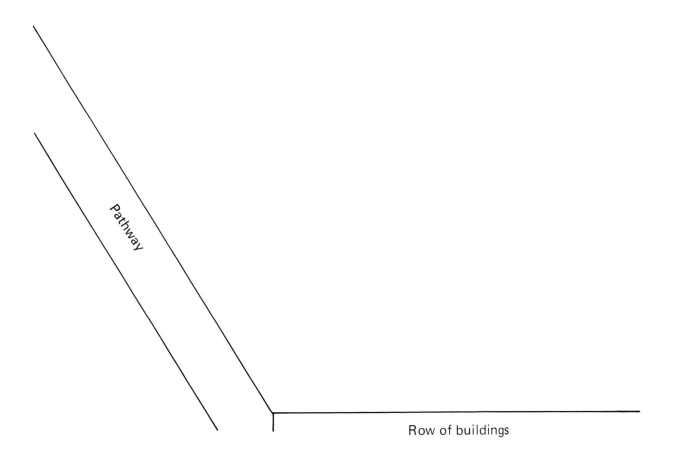

Pathway

Row of buildings

96